From Mom & Pop To Millionaire

9 Steps to Create a Legacy of Wealth

William R Scott Jr.
with **Rita M. Scott**

TABLE OF CONTENTS

www.mompopmillionaire.com

ACKNOWLEDGMENTS

From: Pop

My Sons: Anthony & Michael
Everything I do now makes sense. You are the reasons.

My Mom: Mary Manning
You were my first breath and heartbeat. You are love.

My Dad: William R. Scott Sr.
I hope I made you proud. I love you; rest in peace.

My sisters: Robin Briscoe & Trina Mims
You believed in me even when I didn't.

Randell McShepard, Dave Leone & Craig Manning
Thanks for your friendship in writing this book.

A special thanks to my friend & coach Bob
You unknowingly helped me so much. Thanks!

From: Mom

My parents: Noah & Dolores Monsour
Thank you for always believing in me.

My sisters: Mary Monsour, Amy Schneider
& Sara Binzley
You were my first sorority of love. Thanks!

And of course, Renee Baker, Lisa Miotke & Lisa Leone
For a friendship that is as pure as gold.

FORWARD

Change has been coming toward Americans at break-neck speed since the summer of 2008. The collapse of AIG (American Insurance Group) which precipitated the TARP (Troubled Asset Relief Program) bailout altered the financial climate to a point where most IRAs and 401ks came crashing down. At that moment, it became clear that we could no longer allow the government to be the custodian of our future and our wealth.

I recall talking to my late grandfather about the hard times of the 1930's and 1940's when he was a sharecropper in South Carolina. He said when times got hard; "you returned to the land and worked harder because the land would give you what you needed". He did what he knew, which was to farm and raise live stock to put food on the table. These were times where self-reliance was the norm.

He didn't rely on a payroll check and he knew couldn't rely on unemployment benefits like many do today. He knew he could only rely on himself and his family to have a better life, and because of his work ethic he was able to buy his own farm. After more conversations with Grandpa it became clear that he was the epitome of a true entrepreneur in those early days.

He demonstrated his business acumen in deciding on the best crops to plant, the best farm hands to hire and how to sell his produce at the highest price. His money management skills allowed him to take a portion of his profits to buy more land in order to increase his revenue. Not bad for a man with a sixth grade education.

Though I feel my grandfather was a great man; many in his era made a living on the farm in a similar manner. We were an agrarian nation and this was a major component of our GDP (Gross Domestic Product), and these farmers were business people who took their livelihood into their hands and took care of their families. There is a lesson here on self-reliance that most of us have forgotten.

Too many of us feel that we need a job to make it in life. We put our identity into what we do and we will acquiesce to almost anybody to keep that identity, social position and money. We do this because many of us don't believe that we can be successful relying on ourselves. Many believe that there is less risk in having a job than there is in creating a business. Well, with the true unemployment rate over 20 %; we disagree.

The seeds of entrepreneurship are deeply planted in our cultural DNA; we simply chose not to acknowledge them. We ignore this calling because we are completely sold on the fallacy of our educational system and the resulting career paths derived from it. There is a better way. We hope you accept our invitation to take a life-changing trek on the road of entrepreneurship. And to make this trip even more fun and exciting, we ask you to grab your spouse by the hand and take this road together.

A husband and wife team is an unbeatable combination of nurturing love and driving commitment; both of which are necessary to get to your desired goal. So strap on your seatbelt and grab the steering wheel of your future as we take you down some fun roads, as well as some challenging ones. Because on this trip we guarantee that you will learn much and earn even more. Thanks for letting us sit in the backseat as you drive toward your dream of entrepreneurship. Relax, we know all the mile markers, potholes and exciting sites and we will be your guide for as long as you need us.

Cataloging-in-Publication data for this book is available from the Library of Congress.

ISBN: 9781466420892

REVELATION OF REALITY

"You've got to work twice as hard to get half as much" was the mantra of my mother. She was a divorced mother with three kids doing all she could to keep us out of the troubles of our neighborhood and the Cleveland School System. She worked the night shift at an auto factory to pay the tuition that kept us in catholic schools. She was certain that this would give us the opportunity to achieve the American Dream.

But what was the American Dream? Well, Mom had a hard time finding the words to explain it so she would eventually use this one concise statement; *"The American Dream is anything other than the way we are living now"*. As with most parents of her generation; getting an academic education was the only viable way out of poverty. So she dedicated herself to making sure that we all graduated from good schools and got accepted into good colleges.

My mother was, and is, the personification of beauty and strength to me. Her unconditional loving hand has been guiding me since my first breath and my life is so much better because God gave her to be my mother. Abraham Lincoln summed up my feelings best in his quote, *"All that I am, or hope to be, I owe to my angel mother"*. She fed my stomach, soul and dreams with care.

From the moment I started first grade I completely fell in line with her train of thought because of a few salient reasons. First, she was my Mom and I did what I was told. Second, I never wanted to disappoint the woman I loved so much. And last, but surely not least, I wanted to be rich. My sisters and I were well versed in the vernacular of being poor at an early age because we experienced divorce, bankruptcy, food stamps, turned off utilities and Goodwill stores on a consistent basis. So I concluded that it was paramount to grow up and live like the rich people I've heard so much about.

After graduating from high school, I went on to Baldwin-Wallace College (a small Methodist school in Ohio). For four years I dedicated myself to study and putting myself in the most advantageous position in comparison to my classmates. I started interning with companies as early as my sophomore year and was selected for a work/study program with Hewlett-Packard; working in marketing and sales support.

The job didn't pay a red cent but I knew that it would pay dividends later in my career. My junior year, I hired on with Xerox to perfect my sales skills by selling copiers in 1985. In the 80's, Xerox was the premier company to work for if you wanted to learn how to be a salesman. The indoctrination process taught me that bloody knuckles and holes in the soles of your shoes were like badges of courage in the field of sales.

"I'm putting myself in a position to get out of the gate fast" is what I told my friends when asked why I was so focused. I would tell my fraternity brothers that I was a young, educated black man on the rise. And based on my limited information I thought I was doing the right things to achieve my dreams. Some of the upperclassmen I looked up to took similar paths and received excellent job offers from great companies.

This was the only roadmap to success I had at the time. I couldn't lean on parents who had previously blazed the trail I sought nor could I go to my parent's country club and seek the counsel of other successful club members. There were no 1-on-1s with my family's lawyer, accountant or financial advisor. These may have been the right people to ask for guidance…or maybe not, the problem was that I had no idea. But I was smart and I knew that I could out work anybody, so if I stayed on this uncertain path all things would be revealed to me. This is what I hoped would happen. But as you know; hope is not a good strategy to achieve success.

In 1986, I graduated to start my first full-time sales job with Xerox. What a proving ground for sales success! Xerox could prepare you to sell water to the ocean so I walked out of their training program feeling that I was unstoppable. After achieving President's Club with them, I received a call from Hewlett-Packard to join the sales team they designated to open the Toledo office.

From there, got married to my beautiful bride, later hooked up with a big software company and began to carve out my piece of the American Pie.

What Is The American Dream?

At 22 years old, I knew I had this part nailed down because I had lived the American Dream in my head a million times. It included a huge house on a hill with a picket fence, two luxury cars parked in the garage and luxurious vacations twice a year. And of course, it included a beautiful wife with two kids and a dog.

Sounds familiar I bet? It may even sound a little dated, but this was the dream of just about every young person in 1986. No originality whatsoever because I was in a trance brought on by the mass hypnotic lie. Yes, I said lie. This is the lie that was delivered to all of us in most TV commercials, sitcoms, movies and print ads. It's the lie deeply embedded in our institutional educational system from elementary school to college. It's this system that is incapable of teaching us those things that are most important to our future. Our educational system is not setup to teach us about money, how it works and how you can use it to your advantage.

It is not setup to teach us about key concepts like leverage, cash flow and asset building. No, no no!! The school systems sole purpose is to tell us how to be a good employee, take direction and advance in the corporate world. We are all convinced that this is the golden ring that we should all compete to win. And boy, do we compete. We fight to get on the Dean's List and get accepted to the best universities just for the opportunity to compete for these key jobs.

This reminds me of line from the book entitled *Rich Dad, Poor Dad*. While the author was working hard at Xerox as a young man his rich dad asked him, *"Who are you making rich?"* What a coincidence, because when I worked at Xerox and I was well aware that I was making the shareholders rich; not myself. That is what my schooling had taught me: to do the bidding of my employer (business owners) to make them richer by building their assets and increasing their cash flow, not mind. Not a bad way to make a living, just not a good way to become financially independent.

How many times have you heard the adage: "*Get a college degree so that you can get a good job.*" What was so ironic about this advice is that it's always given to me by poor, financially uneducated (but well meaning) people who wanted the best for me. That was what they were told by others and from their vantage point (outside looking in), it seemed most logical.

This supposed yellow brick road to success was the only advice that I consistently received from family, friends and even strangers. And I always listened. What the heck did I know? These were people seasoned by life so I assumed that along with wrinkles and gray hair followed wisdom on issues such as these. Up to that point, I never received any advice to the contrary; no opposing frame of reference to challenge the status quo had ever presented itself. So I completed my undergraduate education and set off to achieve my American Dream.

But soon there came a fork in the road on my quest for success. I thought that I had the keys to the kingdom when I received a promotion to Director of Sales for a software company. I was making a salary in the mid six figures not including profit-sharing, stock options. This afforded me lavish trips and custom-tailored suits (with my body-type; that was a must). My machismo factor was very high because my career allowed my wife the opportunity to stay home with our 3 year old son and yet have everything that she desired. Trust me ladies when I say this….. Nothing makes a husband feel manlier than when he is providing everything that his wife desires. This is another fallacy that feeds the American Dream.

So let me check my **Life Score** sheet at this point:

Moving up the corporate ladder	*9*
Six-Figure Income	*10*

| *Nice home, cars, vacations* | *10* |
| *Beautiful wife & kid* | *10+* |

Man, I am killing it! But why was I so miserable? This job had my butt strapped to a plane from Sunday afternoon to Friday night; week in and week out. And when I flew home on Friday evenings; I had no energy to spend with my family. It took all Friday evening to decompress from the week's activities only to begin mentally working again on Sunday morning. I was missing out on my son's fun years and losing time with my bride & best friend.

"Hey, stop your belly-aching! There are guys who would kill to be where you are!" That was my self-talk when I started to feel sad and sorry for myself. I cannot count how many times I would arrive to a hotel room to call my son just to hear his voice and say goodnight. I would tell my wife that I loved her and cry myself to sleep each time I hung up the phone.   In and out of 3-4 airports per week would leave my head spinning. They would call me on my cell phone and Anthony would always ask, "Daddy, where are you today?" Most times I wouldn't know, so I would have to look at the receiver on the hotel phone to find the address; what insanity.

And then the weekend homecomings started to become "frosty" with my wife as the years went by. Here is this beautiful, supportive woman who only wanted me and I had no energy to give her what she desired. She was consistently denied what she deserved and she was running out of patience. On one Sunday during the holiday season, before I left for the airport, it became clear that she had enough. I was in my usual distant mood thinking about the coming week's sales calls and making quota before Christmas. She looked me squarely in the eyes and said "*If you cannot have your heart and mind with us when you are here; then don't bother coming home on the weekends*". Those words drove a dagger into my heart and only then did I realize the pain in my wife's soul.

But I justified it by saying that I was the sole provider and she really didn't want to give up the lifestyle that this job afforded us. She constantly reminded me that she would gladly give it up today if

I would just get a job that kept me home. More important, she wanted to have another baby and so did I. If you understand biology, in order to make this happen I couldn't just FedEx it from Memphis; I had to be there to make that happen. But I kept putting it off saying that it would only be for a short while longer until this division got off the ground.

Bent Arrow Determination: My Father's Wisdom

When you are on a path that you've deliberately created it takes a cataclysmic shift in your life in order to change directions. Like an arrow being shot toward its target, my career success was my focus and I was determined to hit my mark. But it was my father that gently took my career arrow and bent it; sending it toward a whole new target. A new target which offered more fulfillment than anything I had ever given my attention. It was with his wisdom that I took every life-arrow in my quiver and bent them toward a goal that was worthy of me and my family.

It will be clear as we move forward that my wife and son were a vital reason for my change in direction, but it was my father that gave me the final push. I share this with you because if you selected this book in order to start a business or grow a business with your spouse, then you must be clear on your motivation. Whatever your reasons to get out of the corporate rat race and become an entrepreneur one thing must be clear; the reason for the transition must be bigger than you. It must be bigger than all your fears, doubts and insecurities. My dad helped me find that as I visited him in a hospital room at the Cleveland Clinic.

I got off a plane in Waukesha, Wisconsin and grabbed a rental car heading to a rendezvous point to meet the people on my sales team for a big sales call. My phone rang and I saw my sister's number pop up. "I don't have time right now Sis" was my greeting to her. "I hate to give you the news this way, but Dad's in the hospital having emergency surgery due to an infection from his Crohn's disease and it looks really bad." I pumped the brakes on my rental car and my life right then and there. I immediately called my VP to inform him that I was headed back to Cleveland ASAP. I assured him that everything would be fine and I would turn around and be in Memphis the following morning.

Dad and my relationship could be defined as the epitome of a love/hate relationship. During my childhood, my parent's divorce was tough on me and it made our father & son relationship very difficult. But when I got married and became a dad myself, he reached out to become a bigger part of my life and we revived our relationship. But lately, I became too busy. No anger or resentment because we both found forgiveness; it was just that I was too damn busy. An occasional call or a drive by "hello" is all I would give him. He had been fighting this disease all his life and now the disease struck a serious blow causing me to fill with regret. I rushed home thinking to myself about all the *"should ofs"* that I let slip by with my dad.

When I arrived, he had been out of surgery for a few hours and was resting in Post Op. It felt weird to see all my family members together because I didn't have time for all the weekend get-togethers that we were invited to. I felt like a stranger near all the people I loved so much. Soon, I was able to see my father and he looked bad. He had multiple tubes going into his body which looked like spokes in a hub.

To my amazement he looked at me with a warm smile. His face didn't show the pain I knew he felt, he just gave me that smile because he could see I needed it. He gave me the greeting that he had given me all my adult life; "How ya' doing Son?" Though at that moment I felt the weight of the world presses upon my shoulders I needed to concentrate on him. My sisters left the room so that I could have some quiet time with dad to make sure that we could air out anything that may have been festering over the years. The looks on their faces made me feel that he didn't have much time.

I wanted to keep it light so as not to upset him, so I asked him what lead up to this episode. "It's the same old song son. Thought I was coming down with the flu bug so I took some medicine and hunkered down in the bed", he said. "I guess I was wrong". He softly spoke of how he hadn't seen me in a while and how he hated to pull me off the road with such an emergency. "I'm sorry that I couldn't be here earlier Dad. I guess this was a wakeup call for me and you", I said.

He mentioned that he got his wake up call years ago. He briefly described his regrets in his failed marriage with my mother; a conversation I never thought I would ever have with him. He talked more about the self-pity he felt over his disease and the disconnect he had from his kids for a multitude of reasons. But most emphatically he regretted his choice to work 7 days-a-week in an automobile factory for 8 plus years straight. The toll it took on his family, health and spiritual well being was tremendous. His eyes slowly began to fill with tears and I was taken aback because I've rarely witnessed such a moment with my father. I've never seen my father's tears.

Was he cleansing his soul with me because he felt that his last moments were approaching? I was not willing to be his confessor nor was I going to allow him to "check out" on us in this hospital bed. We forgave our dad in this matter years ago, but I must admit it took years to reach that point.

"Why are you telling me this now", I whispered. "These are the lowest points in my life's journey and though I've always known what was most important, I always let the world distract me. I wanted the dream to be real too, just like you've always said son", he said. My dad felt he spent too much time on things that didn't matter as much; like working hard. Time spent at work in lieu of a relationship with his family was the mistake. So he wanted more for his children; more choices. Mom & dad always wanted us to get the best education possible in order to secure our future. And for two high school graduates from the south, they managed to raise three children with college degrees and two of them with MBAs. This made them most proud.

But even on his near-death bed, dad could not resist the opportunity to teach me something. I've always been a "hard headed kid" as they always said, so it's no surprise that I would listen to his preaching with one ear. After a long but comfortable silence, dad said to me "Should I be worried about you"? Worried about me! I'm not the one lying in a hospital bed with deadly poison leaking from his intestines and a fever as high as the surface of Mercury! Was this delirium, the medication or was he talking from a higher spiritual place brought on by the surgery?

I had to reassure him that I was okay so that we could both concentrate on him and his health. "Business is great" I said with a quiet confidence. "How are Rita and my grandson" was his next casual question. "Well she's not happy with my travel, but she wants to start a new business and needs me to buy a building. Maybe if she has something to do she will get off my back and give me more affection when I'm home on the weekends," was my narrative.

"You bought her a building? That's a great way to show confidence in your wife's dream" dad said. "May I ask you how much something like that cost you?" This was an odd question from my dad; he never asked about my finances. I described how I negotiated the deal and got below the asking price, etc., all the while building myself up as smart and crafty businessman. Even in my late 30s, I'm still trying to win my father's approval.

"I understand Anthony is taking karate?" was his next probing question. I mentioned that Anthony shown interest in basketball, football, baseball and karate and that I signed him up for lessons and camps in all four sports to nurture his desires. Most of these events happen during the week so I couldn't be there.......that really hurt.

"All those lessons must set you back quite a bit?" he said in the clearest tone of the conversation. Again, he asked another uncharacteristic financial question. I told him about this particular facility that offered most of the lessons which allowed me to negotiate a deal based on the number of classes taken. I was proud to negotiate this so Rita wouldn't have to drive all over the city. He was proud that I was succeeding in my career and I could afford to give my family all they wanted.

"But I wish that I could be there for Anthony. I sometimes feel that I'm missing out on his childhood," was all that I muttered. "Sometimes the price you pay for corporate success is measured by your relationship with your family & friends." he said. Now, that was the Dad I knew. He maybe in the hospital in a sicken state but he still could not resist the urge to coach, coerce and taunt me on these life issues.

"What are you trying to say dad? I work hard to give my family everything they could want. She gets to stay home and raise our son, hang out with her friends and decorate the house in any fashion she deems fit. And you're trying to make me feel bad about my success?" I said with an elevated tone.

"No son, I'm trying to make you aware that you were feeling bad about this long before we started the conversation because you feel disconnected. I'm proud of how far you've come but I'm scared of what you've become. You put so much emphasis on climbing the corporate ladder and providing for your family that you've lost sight of your true treasures from God: your wife and son."

"I've listen closely to you about your six-figure earnings and how you are paying the price for success. And I've listened of your prowess in negotiating a lower price on the building as well as my grandson's lessons. You have proven your skill in understanding the real price of the things you want in your life, but I'm still worried about you son", he said with a sad voice.

Now we have come full circle because this conversation began with him stating his worry for me. At this point, I was getting pretty upset because this hospital visit wasn't supposed to be about me; it should be about him. "I don't want to be disrespectful nor give you anymore pain than what you are experiencing because of the surgery, but you are not making sense," was my reply.

"Ok, the question is this and it's rhetorical so a reply is not necessary. But before I pose the question, let's get some facts straight. First, you have a wife who loves you dearly and wants you in her life. Secondly you have a son who needs your guiding and loving hand and wants you with him. Not to mention the fact that Rita wants another child and the things you promised her as a husband has been put on hold."

"Now let's look at the other side of the page. You've been promoted from a sales rep to Director of Sales at a rapid pace. You make well over six-figures and get to see all of America through your travels. This great job gives you lots of money and perks but no time with your family. Not to mention what the dining out every night, hotels and airports is having on your body and health. You have now become an expert in negotiation so you can lower your costs. So when you get to the bottom line the questions is: *What has your success cost you?*

My mind went totally blank and the room became silent. My dad's eyes looked into mine as to probe my soul for the answer he had already known. My feet became cold instantly; I had just been found out by a man who knew me my whole life. The façade that I thought was pristine was merely a silk screen vale to him and I wasn't fooling anybody….not even myself. It became very apparent that the life change that we desired must start today.

He grabbed my hand and asked me to remember. Remember what I already knew was most important in my life. He said *"You must surrender the chase of those things you can never possess in order to gain those things you can never lose."* I quietly sat there slowly internalizing what he had said. I understood clearly what he wanted me to remember. The corporate world's prizes were an ever eluding illusion. I had to surrender them in order to gain something I could never loss; my self respect and the love of my family.

A NEW ERA: CONTINUOUS CHAOS

Today in 2011, we began the year with unemployment over 9.5% with real estates values dropping like a rock. With food and energy prices reaching ever new highs it has gotten to where our incomes can no longer keep pace. Today's newscasts are focused on the people in the Middle East (Tunisia) who are rioting against the current regime. "Give Us Sugar!" they cry because these people have been reduced to their most basic need: food. And in our American arrogance, we think such a dilemma could never reach our shores. Do we really believe this to be true or are we just denying the prospect of such an occurrence because we are Americans? I feel very sad for those who refuse to wake up.

When this change started in early 2007 it was considered, by most, to be a normal contraction in our economy because up & down cycles must be expected. We were told by the mainstream media that this economic malaise was no different than a weather storm. One of the anchors on CNBC used this analogy so as not to alarm their viewership of the impeding dangerous new territory this country was heading toward.

A mere "storm in a teacup" or "not a big deal" they would say. They want you to believe that the US has seen this before and we will get through it just as we did in the past. But this financial storm is much different than past storms. And even more important is that these unfolding events have never been seen before at anytime in this young country's past. Well, let's talk about the anatomy of a weather storm to see if there are any similarities to present day economic events.

First, a weather storm can be forecasted by a meteorologist with a high degree of predictability and accuracy. So to continue the comparison, this financial storm should have been predicted by the economists well before it hit. But the reality is that the economic storm clouds rolled in and the economist had no idea that there was no sunlight. Or if they did now they decided not to warn us. Most of them had no inkling that the storm was upon us until we were blown away by the highest winds of the financial hurricane in late 2007.

Reports came out stating that we were in a recession a full 6 months after the financial storm began. If a weather person got on TV to announce that a storm is coming a full day after it had past; then that poor weather person would be run out of town or tarred and feathered at the very least. This announcement hit the airwaves in the 2nd quarter of 2008 that the current recession started in the 4th quarter of 2007; it was too late to make adjustments. They failed to recognize data in job reports, inventory levels and housing starts all of which were sloping downward in the beginning of 2007. They also ignored the fact that our low interest rate policy made investment speculation easier for all people. How's that for their ability to forecast?

Second, a weather storm's intensity can be measured and accurately forecasted. How many miles the storm will stretch, how fast is it moving, wind speed and rain fall and snow accumulation are all within the realm of their predictability. That's because of all the technical instruments a weather person has at his disposal like satellites and Doppler radar. But during our financial storm, economist would have us believe that this so-called "recession" would be mild due to the liquidity in the market and the incentives for businesses to invest and grow. One would think that with all their tools to measure all relevant indices in the market that we would have received similar accuracy in how this financial storm would affect our day-to-day lives.

Well, the housing market was beginning to show some chinks in its armor early in 2007. But that was merely put off as a non-issue because the market could absorb the excess inventory due to the money moving from lenders to the people. But the Federal Reserve knew something was wrong because they kept interest rates low. Easy money became the preferred way to get wealthy for the past 10 years because this made it easy for speculators to use excess leverage to buy assets.

And they were buying assets fast at any price just looking forward to the appreciation in a few short years. This was the precursor to the real estate bubble. So as we sat through this economic malaise it became apparent that our government leaders were either inept or just not telling us the truth.

Lastly, even a mediocre meteorologist can give you a pretty good idea as to when the storm will end. When a storm hits our part of the Midwest, we can simply look at the Weather Channel and via satellite see the storm's movement. We can tell within minutes, or hours, when the storm will pass. That is the proper use of technology and critical instruments to monitor a storm. The government continued to give job reports and economic forecasts that were "not as bad as predicted" and then they will revise prior quarter data to show improvement. All with the intent of giving us the elusion that things are getting better; but they were not.

And then the financial analyst from the big investment banks perpetrate the same fraud by giving "buy" recommendations on certain industries and stocks using the same erroneous data supplied by government officials. These inconsistencies prove that no one had any idea of the severity of this storm or when it would end. And the Federal Reserve was showing their confusion as well. They were running out of ink printing so much money for TARP and QE (Quantitative Easing) & QE2. They too were beginning to panic because there were no growth prospects on the horizon.

So, the comparison of our current economic situation to a storm is a banal and trite description that goes far deeper. And it is a major insult to the intelligence and integrity of every American who needs to know the truth because we have never seen this kind of storm before. It defies most of the rules and laws that apply to financial storms we've seen in the past (i.e. the Great Depression and the Stagflation of the 1970's). If we are to make today's situation analogous to a storm it would be more like the intensity of Hurricane Katrina with winds far higher than anything ever recorded. It would be so wide that it would not only cover the whole USA, but all industrialized nations. And based on current models we would forecast the storm rolling back out to sea …….. NEVER. This will be our continuous chaos.

Old Playbook vs. New Playbook

I paint this picture not to scare you but to motivate you. No longer can we win the game of life using the old playbook because the game of life has changed. We have to take the helm of the future and guide it toward our own goals for success. Here are some old plays that were successful a decade ago, but will surely have you lose The Game of Life today:

The Old Playbook	The New Playbook
Go to college so that you can get a good job.	Get a financial education so you can build a business.
Get out of debt ASAP.	Leverage debt to get ahead.
Your house is the best investment for the future.	Invest in assets for cash flow now and in the future.
Save your money for the future.	Trade money for cash flowing assets that will outpace inflation
Invest in stocks, mutual funds & bonds	Acquire the knowledge to manage your own investments

Traditional Education vs. Financial Education

As we mentioned in an earlier part of the book; getting a college education will not serve you as well as it did in the past. Today's continuous chaos demands more of you in order to be successful in reaching your dreams. As of 2010, many college grads started their first job doing something that they didn't trained for in school. Because of the economy, they take temporary jobs in the service sector (waiters, cooks, landscaping etc) in order to make ends meet. They've been forced to stay home with their parents because it's too hard to make a living at these income levels while paying back their college loans.

College now appears to be a luxury reserved only for the rich with tuition prices outpacing annual inflation by 5-to-1 at some institutions. The sad reality today is that a student graduating from college with a Bachelor of Arts degree has elected, by default, to jump head first into a death spiral of debt. The average student in 2009 received their four year degree from the president of their university only to get a bill from the bursar's office that will be around $30k to $70k. And this is after financial aid. When I graduated in 1986, I had over $20k in college loans with a base salary of $24k. At that time I felt it was a mountain that would be hard to climb, so today's graduate must be feeling the same way.

This is not how our young envisioned the start of their American Dream with an average of $50k in debt before they get their first job. And for most graduates, their first job will only yield an annual income that will be a fraction of the outstanding debt of their college loan. So if you've landed a job making any income; you should consider yourself lucky. Our niece was not as lucky, after graduating with honors she has yet to find a job nine months later.

Let's move this scenario forward a bit to demonstrate how this debt can overcome you. Let's say you've got your college degree and your first job. And you want to marry your sweetheart and buy your first home. This could happen if you are fortunate enough to qualify for a home loan. And if you do, you will find yourself with another $125k or so in mortgage debt on top of your college debt. I forgot to mention your monthly payment for some reasonably priced cars. Ok, let's do a quick tally; you are in your late 20's with potentially over $200k in debt. Are you overwhelmed yet?

Hey, you don't need the house or the nice cars, but this was the dream you were sold since your early years. And a college education was the key to the American dream; you have the degree now you want the dream. Now the bitter pill you must swallow is that you have to pay for the degree, house and car; month in and month out. At the end of the month, you are now handing over a majority of your disposable income to someone else.

If this current cycle of exponential tuition increases continues in higher education, the new bubble will be student loans with defaults reaching the stratosphere. Did I mention that bankruptcy will no longer protect you from the consequences of a college loan default? This system is not setup for your success and it never will be. This process fills the pockets of the banks and the education institutions and makes you a financial slave to them for a majority of your young life. I think you would agree when I say that none of us decided to go to college to become indentured servants.

That's the old playbook that will no longer serve you. The best play in this situation is to get a financial education in conjunction with a traditional education. College doesn't teach us about money and debt and how we can have them work to serve us. I find it amazing that one of the smartest guys I went to undergrad with moved on to become a plastic surgeon and is currently in dire financial straits. All because he never learned how to make his considerable income work for him so he could secure his future. You probably know someone like this or it could be you.

He bought the biggest house in the best neighborhood, as well as a summer home in Florida. He leases luxury cars for him and his stay-at-home wife and bought a fractional ownership in a jet so he could avoid the hassle of commercial airline travel. If he had put as much effort in his financial literacy as he put into his medical training, he would of developed assets that could pay for all the homes and cars without any extra effort on his part.

The major disease of every American is that we are dying slowly of excessive consumption; some faster than others. We are consuming more than we can afford with the operative word being afford. Let me say this, we are proponents of having all you desire which is the fuel that feeds the dream of success. But we come from the school of thought that you must make your business and assets pay for your luxuries, not your earned income. You can have all you want but you must make sure that your assets make more than enough to cover it.

Our country is in desperate need of financial education on how money works to make wealth. The upside is that this education does not take place in a traditional classroom as does a college degree (I never liked the classroom). And it can pay dividends to you and your family for generations to come. Key accounting, financial and investment concepts are the stepping stones to a lifetime of wealth. Coupled with good coaching and a strong conviction; your dreams can be reality.

The genesis of this education is in how you should view money. Think of each dollar you earn as another worker bee that you are adding to your colony of assets. And like a worker bee, each dollar is responsible for bringing nectar back to your hive in order to make honey…or should I say money. And a part of that worker bee's job is to make more worker bees to add to the colony, this is how dollars make more dollars. Make your money work harder than you work for your money.

Leveraging the Proper Debt

Rita and I are firm believers in using the right leverage to get to our desired situation and debt is an important component in making that happen. Learning the right amount of leverage and how to use it in all business situations is what separates the eternal wealthy from the "flash in the pan". I've heard many people from the Depression Era say that debt will be the death of our society; they are both right and wrong in this viewpoint. Debt is a tool that if used properly will serve you well by creating cash flow, but when used in a cavalier manner; will kill you financially.

Most American households are swimming in consumer debt that is in the multiples of their annual income; this is the bad debt. They used their home-equity as an ATM machine to finance things like new cars, home improvements and vacations. This is unsustainable and unwise. You must do all you can to de-leverage yourself of consumer debt because it has no financial advantages to it. But there are financial advantages to commercial and investment debt that makes money for you, not to mention the tremendous tax advantages available as well.

I equate debt to a rope dangling from high a top your mountain of success. There are many ropes of leverage that you will need to master in order to make it to the top, but in our eyes, debt is the most crucial. So to continue this analogy; this "debt rope" stretches from the heights of our biggest dreams down to the valley of our humble beginnings where we all start our journey.

If we are not educated properly, we will grab that rope and struggle to scale the mountain to reach the top; and I do mean struggle. If we fail in using this tool properly, the outcome could be business failure and maybe even bankruptcy. This would be like accidentally wrapping the rope around your neck and hanging to your death. Not a very pretty sight, but that's the outcome we've seen far too many times in America with less than half of all new businesses making it to their second year of operation.

It's important to say that some people get ahead of themselves when using debt. Some take on projects, buildings and or equipment purchases that put undue strain on the business. These people were negligent with their due diligence or didn't use the proper professionals for guidance. The end affect is too much debt and not enough revenue. Then there are the others who may have a little success early and decide to reward themselves with a new sports car or a new Rolex……nice. This could be a Venus Fly Trap that pulls you in and slowly kills you.

We say a great business is similar to a child. In the beginning, you have to do everything for the child so that it can survive. That means you become the jack of all trades doing what is necessary to get this business off the ground. Soon, your child matures and she can take care of her basic needs with some guidance from you on the important stuff. Similar to the business; you will still need to offer your leadership and vision at this stage. You hire the right people, put great systems in place and the business runs itself successfully with less oversight from you on the day-to-day stuff.

Your child is now an adult reaching the pinnacle of her profession; flushed with cash. She wants to buy her momma a house and because she is successful, she does it without disturbing any obligations to her own house. What a good daughter! Well, a successful business is like the daughter in that it can reward you too with nice things without missing a step on its path of profitability.

Now back to my rope analogy. With the proper use of debt, the rope becomes a very strong and stable tool capable of pulling your company to the mountain top. It provides the proper fail-safes to stop you from falling to your financial death. This leverage also gives you other benefits that will get you to your destination in a fraction of the time it would have taken using just your resources. Even if you borrowed from family and friends it still pales in comparison to the advantages of borrowing from a bank.

Rita & I learned the power of debt through one of our friends/coach when we sought to build our second school. It was new construction and he taught us to use the cash flow from our current school to leverage a new school. We found a bank that lent us 90% of the money to build with the down payment spread out over twelve draws during the construction period. Because we learned the power of debt, we were able to have two schools' monthly debt service paid for by the cash flow of just one.

And more importantly, when the second school began making revenue, we had much more cash in our pockets to support our lifestyle. The beauty of debt used properly is that we control the property and get all the write-offs of depreciation, taxes, interest and maintenance. And the bank only asks that the business pays the debt service on time. This is how debt makes us money.

Understanding Cash Flow

My parents were firm believers that their home was their biggest asset because that was the message the government gave us via tax deductions. And for them, and all the other baby-boomers, it worked out fine because the homes appreciated quite a bit. My childhood home was purchased in 1973 for $19k and sold in 2003 for $89k. Not a bad payday for a home in a less-than-desirable part of town.

Mom thought she made a pretty good profit so she used it to downsize her residence. The old home became too much to maintain and had far too much room for a single grandmother. She moved to a better part of town, reduced her living space by more than half and reduced exterior upkeep because it was a townhouse with a maintenance fee. She went into this venture thinking she would lower her cost of living as well….. Not even close. Even after putting a major down payment on the new townhouse, her living expenses doubled through taxes, mortgage payments, maintenance fees, insurance etc.

She no longer looks at a home as an investment for the future; it just sucks all your money away. She said that <u>you should buy the house you like and can afford and not consider it an investment, because it's not</u>. We learned early through reading and listening to audio books that we would only invest in properties that made a monthly cash flow. Shelter is necessary and a nice house is very desirable. We love our house but we don't fool ourselves into thinking that it's an asset because everyday it costs us money.

The new playbook says to invest in things that generate cash flow and that process starts long before you purchase the asset. Doing your homework and consulting experts will allow you to receive a monthly revenue stream that will not only pay for the asset, but also pay for your lifestyle. Chances are that one asset alone will not pay for your desired lifestyle, so you must constantly add to your portfolio using your proven due diligence process.

I recall the first rental house that we bought as we made our first attempt to become real estate kings. We thought we were smart in buying a condo in a town that was growing at a 12% clip each year. The property was new construction (mistake #1) and we bought it from the developer at list price (mistake #2). We rented it out immediately at the going rental rate in that town. After all expenses, we were netting only $21 a month.

What the heck went wrong? Well, we had not yet learned the supreme rule for investment properties which is your: *Cash flow level is determined by the manner in which you acquire the property.* It's not only the price but financing, neighborhood, terms of the agreement and unrealized value that are all critical points. We were unaware of these things in that first deal. Suffice it to say, our next deal was far more profitable giving us a cash-on-cash return of 24.5%. Look at the deal.

$$Cash\text{-}on\text{-}cash\ return = \frac{Annual\ Before\text{-}Tax\ Cash\ Flow}{Total\ Cash\ Invested}$$

We put $9k on a $90k house and cleared $183.90/month after all expenses, which is $2,207/year. This gave us a COC return of 24.5%; in little more than 4 years we had our cash returned to us. We made monthly cash flow with the bank's money; not ours.

$$\frac{\$2,207}{\$9,000} = 24.5\%\ \ COC\ return$$

We mentioned this real estate deal to show you a real life example of good cash flow. Never pay retail for an asset because you immediately decrease your cash flow potential. This can apply to buying a business, a piece of equipment, a building, a rental house, etc. Stay away from investments that place value on esthetics unless the numbers makes sense.   Don't be swayed by new construction, like a new home or new office building, because those assets are always sold at a premium markup.

Saving Money is Futile

My first life coach drilled this concept in my head for years. This maybe true for you as well but I knew of no other technique accept saving money and being thrifty in order to become a wealthy person. He would say that *"You don't have to think when saving money that is why it's a no-brainer. Only brainless people save money."* Saving is so simple that you can train a monkey to do it, so if you want to live your life on a banana diet, just continue to save. He loves to live his life with all the nice things: great vacations, collectible cars, nice watches, and he did it with ease and no financial worries. He always had his money working because he knew saving was for sleepwalkers. Only ill-informed people would waste their time with passbook accounts and the like.

In today's environment, you can only make money utilizing the movement of money. That is when money is being lent by banks, invested by business and products are being sold. This is how money can be made. He taught me to keep my money moving and working so it can make more money. First lesson from Richard was to learn to keep other people's money moving to make money for you and your family. I heard this many times on audio tapes and business books but I only used the concept at its most elementary level until Richard entered our lives.

In 2007, we brought a deal to Richard to see if the deal had enough merit to move forward. He would normally guide us on deals and would even invest with us if the deal fit his model for cash flow and control. This particular opportunity entailed two office buildings and one that was about to break ground. Rita and I thought that we should do this deal but we didn't have enough money. We need the down payment on the existing building and the new construction. Our current assets didn't have a lot of equity so we thought we would have to tap our retirement funds to play in this game.

Even though Richard agreed to help us through this deal, I got cold feet and felt that the deal was too big for me. All he said to me was "If everything is in place to move forward and you still feel it's not right… Well, it's just not right." The proper preparation and due diligence would take the emotions out of the equation and you would be compelled to move because the numbers were right. If I didn't "feel right" it was because I hadn't properly done my homework and as usual he was right.

But it was right for him and he moved on the deal himself, with our consent, all the while letting me shadow him through the process. What a valuable lesson to be somewhat of a flunky for a guy who made his fortune in real estate and allowed me to hangout because I brought him into a deal. What I found amazing is that he didn't use his own money for any of this transaction. Yet he gained control of all three buildings with monthly cash flows that covered his personal rate of return. Let me tell you how he did it.

He took a $115k line-of-credit out on one of his apartment buildings and got the banks to agree on 5% down to acquire control of two existing office buildings. Because of the buildings appraisal, as well as the current cash flow from the existing tenants in the buildings; 5% was all that was necessary. He then waited 4 months and took the accumulated cash flow from the existing buildings to fund the building of the new facility. He got the bank to agree upon a 10% down payment on each construction loan draw eliminating the need for a lump sum down payment. The monthly debt payment on the construction loan was covered by the incoming lease payments of the two existing buildings.

It took 16 months to build and that included 11 draws in which he was on the hook for 10% of each draw. He paid it from the rents and still had money in his pocket. In two years, he has a vacancy rate of 8% (92% of the units are leased out) and he is thoroughly drenched in cash. Walking through this transaction with him gave me the knowledge and courage to build our second school using the methodology he showed us.

He would always point out that he didn't have to save a single dime in order to get the deal. And if he had the mentality of "*I have to save enough money in order to do this deal*", well the deal would of just past him by. Besides, the amount we could earn in a savings account or money market account would be quickly eroded by today's inflation. For example, if gas & food prices are increasing at a 4% annual rate and your savings account is paying an annual rate of 1.5%, how are you winning? But if you put that money in a rental home with a great cash flow and a cash-on-cash return of 24.5%, well now we know who is winning.

Be clear that if you become financially literate, you will make more with the movement of money than you could ever make sitting in a savings account. Don't waste your time saving money for a rainy day; put your money to work now.

Take Control of Your Investments

The old way of thinking says take your hard earned money, give it to a broker and let them invest in stocks, bonds and mutual funds. I thought that way in the beginning and lost a lot of money because I was not properly educated. Oh let me get real….. I was too lazy to get properly educated just like many other working stiffs. I spent all my damn energy hustling in sales making the money and now I have to spend more time learning to manage and invest it. Why not just leave it to the professionals, correct? Wrong.

During the late 1980's leading up to the Y2K boom, you could make money in the market fairly easily with minimal risk. Just open up a Kiplinger's or Money Magazine, or any other financial rag, whisk through the pages and pick a mutual fund. Nothing scientific to it; just pick a fund that had a fairly good track record over the last few years. And presto, you were making money in your mutual fund in short order. I opened a mutual fund account as a vehicle to save for the purchase of a house and then opened up another to roll over my 401k; looked at my statement each month and smiled all the way to the bank.

Then the 2000 stock boom came to a bust (as do all bubbles) and it wasn't so easy anymore. You see, I had been so distracted with making a living that I didn't give these accounts the attention they needed. I kept thinking that these were the experts and they knew what they were doing so don't worry. But when I pulled my nose from the grindstone, I realized that I had lost more than 27% of my initial investment's value. I told myself the same crap my broker said which was "invest for the long term". So I needed to hang in there and wait for the market to turn.

Well it turned, alright…it turned from bad to worse with us losing an additional 14% within 12 months. And the kicker was that the brokerage firm kept charging me a fee (commission) when they kept losing money. Let me get this right, I'm going to pay them a fee for the privilege of losing my money? What an education!

Today, you have to take the time to learn how to invest. There are many forms of investment, but in this section we are going to focus on financial instruments. Take classes on investing in stocks and ETFs so you can use 'stops' to reduce your downside. And learn to properly use leverage of options to make monthly cash flow. Once you learn and practice, your confidence will grow and so will your finances. In addition to stocks and options, please learn about commodities.

Commodities are where the new wealth will be found for the remainder of this decade. As we write this cotton, sugar, copper, corn have all experienced a 100%+ gain over 2009 prices. And with the consistent devaluation of the US dollar we have seen oil gold and silver reach all time highs. Let me warn you of the risks associated with commodity trading; the proper training and temperament is crucial. I cannot stress enough the importance of education and coaching when doing this.

The new playbook says that we are responsible for the financial future of ourselves and our children. Rita and I made our declaration early on that we will not let the government dictate our financial situation. We don't give advice on what you should do, so we will only tell you what we've done as of 2002. Money is made out of thin air by central banks all over the world, including the US Federal Reserve. Because of this we believe that the US dollar is becoming worthless in the eyes of the world. So we are finding ways to protect the purchasing power of our currency.

We are invested in oil, agriculture and mining companies as well as currency from countries that are more financially stable than the US. We are still in the stock market today but we are very selective of the industry and companies. And when we take a position on a stock we are very clear on the timing of our exit. We are purchasing gold & silver because it has been money since the days Jesus.

We don't like having the precious metals in our home, as a matter of fact; we don't even want to have our metals in the United States. And please don't put it in a bank's safe deposit box because if our country continues to drown in debt, you will discover it no longer belongs to you. Uncle Sam will need it and claim it. We keep them in segregated vaults in Zurich and Hong Kong safely away from the eyes and hands of the federal government. In these places, it can be safely converting into currency when needed (like Swiss Francs). Though we are not as concerned about a repeat of the Nationalization of Gold that took place in the 1930s, we still believe in protecting our investment from a very desperate Uncle Sam. Study the value of off-shoring some of your assets as well.

But if you decide to have the metals on premise, we recommend three important things: 1.) Get a strong BF rated safe like Gardall & AMSEC, 2.) Don't tell anyone about your metals but your spouse; I mean no one. 3.) Buy firearms and learn how to use them! If things get really bad you must protect your family and your assets. A man without a job and a hungry family will do things that maybe out of his character; desperate things.

Mom & Pop's Key Points:

1. The economic climate has changed so we need better tools, better strategies and better execution.
2. Education in finance & investing is crucial.

Mom & Pop's To Do's:

3. Refresh yourself on basic accounting principles by taking a course at your local community college.
4. Attend a weekend seminar on investing in real estate, stocks, options & commodities
5. Learn how precious metals could preserve your purchasing power. Not numismatic coins; only bullion. This is not an investment; just a way of maintain the value of your current dollars.
6. Learn to grow some of your own organic foods and keep a six month supply of food stored away
7. Take a course in handling fire arms. It's your Second Amendment right and you must learn to use it.

THE BEGINNING - YOUR WEALTH LOGIC

Most people feel that ambition and desire alone are the basis for starting a new business. History has shown that these are important, yet excellent coaching and sound planning are far more valuable. I wanted to find a way to invite the concept of success into this book without talking about the same things you've read in other books...well, it's just not possible. So let's put a frame around this so as to make it easier as you travel down the road of success.

The framework for success starts with understanding your mindset when it comes to being wealthy. I mean being wealthy beyond your wildest dreams. You may say that it's easy to envision yourself with wealth but many have a hard time seeing themselves in the middle of that picture. We've talked to many couples who couldn't see themselves inside the house of their dreams or behind the wheel of their dream car. They couldn't mentally put themselves in that place where they could feel it, smell it, taste it or even see it in their mind's eye. In each case, they had developed a mental block; made of granite ten feet thick. For others, their mindset was just a twisted, perverted view of reality that they weren't truly aware of until confronted with its existence.

Your mindset is crucial and in this book it may be referred to as *thought-set*. This is the invisible luggage that you bring into every wealth opportunity that comes your way. It's invisible to the naked eye, but like luggage it can be very heavy because within its contents you can find every fear and self-doubt you've ever imagined. And again, like luggage, most likely it's been handed down to you by parents or other people you know. Suffice it to say the original thought-set you have wasn't conceived by you, yet you own it just the same.

You've had it for a very long time and it's very recognizable to you among all the other mindless chatter that goes through the conveyor belt of your mind. But unlike real luggage that seems to be easily misplaced by our friendly airlines, these thought-sets are always present and in the forefront of our minds. We must actively get rid of them, redefine them or minimize them in order to diminish its power.

We make this point as we begin this chapter because it was our thought-set that prohibited us from taking our assets over the million dollar hurdle as quickly as we wanted. Keep in mind that I got my wealth frame of reference from the people in my circle of influence: family and friends. In essence, I got my roadmap to wealth from the poorest people I knew; this is what we call a **Perverted Wealth Logic**. It's a tragic loop of beliefs that will only lead you along a labyrinth from which you've come….the hamlet of the poor.

Your PWL not only distorts the reality of being wealthy but it also lays out the fertile ground for many obstacles; namely doubt, hesitation and insecurity. Until you change your thought-set you are destined to stay in a cycle of poverty. Oh, you may fall into momentary success but then your PWL will pull you back and somehow sabotage any ground you may have gained. Your desire to be wealthy is in constant battle with these old thoughts to the point you may become immobile. This immobility is brought on by doubt, "Should I do this? What if this doesn't work? People will call me a failure." Then there are those who become apprehensive and delay doing those very important things necessary to launch a new endeavor. From these people I hear things like "they've stolen my idea", "I designed the same product last year but I didn't think it would sale" or "I guess I was just too late".

Though my family and friends had the best intentions when guiding me, they had no experience, credentials nor success in going from poor to rich. They were inflicted with the same PWL disease and its contagious nature touched all within their sphere. This PWL also comes from looking at the veneer of the wealthy and how they live their lives; what do you normally see? Through the lens of the poor they see a big car, big house, nice clothes, etc. So that must be the definition of being rich because this is what they spend their money on.

But it's an illusion; we only see the material things and not the process that lead to those things. As a great magician once said, "Keep your eye on the other hand". The other hand that I'm referring to is their wealth logic. And just like a good magic trick, you cannot recreate it unless you have knowledge of what the eyes cannot see. It's the process that leads to material wealth and the logic that leads to a successful process. That process begins with the proper thought-set or wealth logic.

Unlike the dinner table of my youth where we talked about sporting events and sometimes other people, I discovered that my wealthy classmates discussed something totally different at the dinner table when they were young. They talked about business, investments and money and how money works. The discussions became more in depth when the parents invited business colleagues, associates and other professionals to the dinner table.

I guess my family would have done the same but we didn't have much money to talk about. We talked about how bad the economy was and how there weren't any good jobs to be had. We blamed our situation on those sons-of-a-bitch Republicans and rich people who were doing everything to keep us down; this was the genesis of my PWL. This thought-set made many of us the victims in every situation and somehow absolved us of taking ownership of our own future.

So this is where many of us had to fight our way out of the hole of poverty. We tried hard to do all the right things; get the right education, surround ourselves with good people, etc. And yet most could not make their dream of success a reality. Now, I have a few friends who've gone from "rags to riches" and had no problem getting past the mental hurdle of their PWL. After many conversations, and observations, we have uncovered a few key steps that these people took to de-program themselves of a thought-set that didn't serve them. We will dedicate much focus to just this at a later time.

To uncover the degree to which your thought-set is holding you back, or propelling you forward, ask yourself the following questions below. Please keep in mind that we want you to get in touch with your feelings and emotions as you read each question. Outside of your family, there is nothing in life that can stir up emotions like money. Let me be more specific; the lack of money.

Please complete the following sentences with the first thing that comes into your mind:

    1.) Money is _____.
    2.) When it comes to money, I am _____.
    3.) When money comes my way, I _____.
    4.) Rich people are _____.
    5.) Growing up, I was taught that money was _____.
    6.) As I watched my parents handle money, I would say they
    _____.

Your answers to these questions will tell you much about your PWL. You may find yourself saying things like, "Money is the root of all evil", "Money is dirty" or "Rich people are just lucky". One of the things that I said early in my maturation process was, "Rich people are rude" and "Rich people are stingy".

If you find yourself making statements like this, its okay; your thought-set is perfectly juxtaposed to where you need to be. This may sound weird but this is the second best place to be other than being totally actualized in the area of wealth and money. It's like having a clean break of the leg compared to a fracture; the former heals with more strength than the latter.

After you determine where you are then you must start the process of re-calibrating your wealth logic; developing tools to refute the logic. An example could be in order to get past your fear of heights you may want to take lessons in parachuting. Sounds extreme but it works because I did just that in college. Re-calibrating my wealth logic was one of the hardest things for me to do (though Rita found it much easier) because I didn't know how to go about it. It was too deeply engrained into my subconscious that it kept popping up and showing itself in many ways.

Whenever I would find myself at a crossroad in business, I would first go to my wife to explain my PWL dilemma to see if we could put our heads together to find a solution. If that didn't yield the desired result, then we would seek a coach. We felt the answer to any PWL roadblock could be found in the mind of a successful person. But at that point in our entrepreneurial lives, we didn't know any wealthy people we could ask to mentor us; so we turned to the bookstore.

We felt like the only way, especially early in this process, to get into the minds and hearts of successful people would be to read some autobiographies, and biographies, of people we hoped to know. Since I wanted to break my PWL about rich people, I chose books about successful rich business people like Steve Jobs, Bill Gates, Robert L. Johnson, Warren Buffett, Oprah Winfrey and Russell Simmons. It became clear to me that though these individuals had great courage, vision and charisma, they weren't that much different than me. Their success didn't make them rude and stingy, but just the opposite. Or could it be that they were never rude or stingy in the first place, just focused and determined.

Then I graduated from wealthy people in books to the real deal when I met a gentleman named Bob. He was my neighbor when I bought my first house after graduating from college. He then became my friend and later my mentor. And well before he became my coach we started a friendship based on our love of sports (primarily fishing), jazz, motorcycles and cars. I never knew much about his line of work other than he worked at a factory. And all he knew about me was that I was in software sales. We felt we didn't need to know anything else because we had our common interests and we liked hanging out.

Then one day I hit a rough patch in my career when the software company that I worked for was sold and I was out of a job. I hit rock bottom emotionally, spiritually and financially and as a friend, he was there with support and encouragement. I recall one day during my unemployment he mentioned that he was taking sometime off to 'recharge his battery" after tough labor union negotiations at work. He was going to the Florida Keys to fish and wanted me to come along.

Now I'm a proud man and I don't need handouts from anyone, and he didn't pose it in that manner. He merely said that he wanted to fish with me and as a friend he wanted to help; isn't that what friends are for? Plus he had a bunch of frequent flyer points he could use to book our tickets. He said that when the world throws him a curve like the one I got; he knew I would have his back. And he was right!

What a life changing trip for me! Not only did I purge myself of the negative residue from being fired but I also got a new zeal for my job search. And as we stood on the deck of this boat casting our fly lines, I for the first time asked Bob detailed questions about what he did for a living. Here was the eye opener for me that totally changed my PWL on money and wealthy people.

First let me describe Bob as a very unassuming guy who is extremely friendly. He has a great sense of humor with a hearty laugh that will make you giggle each time you hear it. As he talked about his work he revealed some startling information; he and his two brothers owned a manufacturing business with multiple facilities throughout the USA.

He also owned office buildings and motels in the Midwest. Are you kidding me? My neighbor was loaded and I didn't know it? How could that be? He lived in a house the same size as mine but I wasn't rich. And though he had two classic cars, his everyday car was nowhere as nice as mine. Talk about the millionaire next door.

He took the two pillars that held up my PWL on rich people and knocked them to the ground crumbling my screwed up thought-set with it. Bob was a rich man and he didn't have a rude bone in his body. He was kind, empathetic and fun to be around. Secondly,

Bob's rich and he's one of the most giving people I've ever met. Not only freely giving himself to me and my family but to other people and causes. But the greatest gift he's given me had nothing to do with his money; it was his knowledge, wisdom and time. It was then I asked him to be my coach and he accepted the job.

Another way we change our PWL about money and rich people was to volunteer. We have volunteered for many different causes like Habitat for Humanity, church groups and different disaster relief activities (i.e. Hurricane Katrina & Rita). And what we found in these organizations were many people who were wealthy business people and public officials willing to dedicate their time and money. We've met many generous people with the conviction and determination to make a difference. It's apparent that these characteristics made them successful, but it was their kindness that made others desire to be in their orbit; just hang around them.

Take time to understand what your early childhood value system has done to form your wealth logic. Then do your homework to understand what is really true and what mere fallacy is. Trust me when I say that if you don't reprogram this part of your logic, it will stand in the way of lasting success and enduring wealth.

Mom & Pop's Key Points:

1. Understanding your PWL will help you discern the incongruity in what you think and what you want.
2. Expanding your circle to include successful people will impact your wealth.

Mom & Pop's To Do's:

3. Read biographies of successful people you admire.
4. In your business dealings; ask yourself what a successful person would do.
5. Join groups and volunteer so you can be around people who are successful at what you want to do.
6. Read these books by Spencer Johnson, MD: "Who Moved My Cheese?" & "Peaks & Valleys". It will assist in understanding your thoughts and how they serve you.

MARRIAGE/BUSINESS COVENANT

I fell in love with Rita at first sight. Word about her came to me when we were in college via a group of female students who resided in my dorm. I was a Residential Assistant (RA) on an all boys floor and occasionally talked to these ladies as I made my rounds. One evening while walking down their floor, I stopped in one of the rooms where about 8 ladies were hanging out.

They told me about how they created a fictitious soap opera set on our college campus and that I played a character in this drama. Based on my virtuous character and pious attitude (not really), I was cast as a man leaving the priesthood and falling for a nun leaving the convent. Of course, Rita was that nun. The pivotal scene this month was us getting together to get married.

I found it amusing but didn't give it much thought until one day in the Student Union another student pointed her out to me. I thought she was cute and decided to use the soap opera idea to introduce myself. Now, let me remind you that I was like most 20 year old men at that time; I felt I could charm any lady.

So I walked up to where she stood in line and said the words "Hello, I'm William Scott and I am your husband." Here I am thinking that she was well aware of this soap opera situation and had heard about me from the girls in the dorm….but that wasn't the case. So here is what happened next; she looked up to me with her beautiful brown eyes and said…..absolutely nothing. Not a blink or a smile just a look of bewilderment. She promptly grabbed her milk and food tray and darted from the line post haste.

This wasn't just egg on my face; this was a Texas-sized western omelet. I really wanted to get to know her but I surely didn't make a great first impression. Though I had a chance to see her on campus a few times after that day, I never approached her again. Thank God that a few months later she approached me to let me know that she just found out about the soap opera and now understood what I was talking about. I should say that the rest is history.

I tell this short story of how we began our relationship because most of our romantic relationships started in some similar fashion, but never our business partnerships. Romantic relationships are initially based on physical attraction and that has no place in a business partnership. Romantic relationships are entered into by leading with your heart and business partnership should be entered into by leading with your head.

Well, we say that the two relationships can be brought together to make a very successful union in life. We've heard people say, "I don't know how you two do it? I would have killed my wife by now if we were in business together". Or "I can't get him to do anything around the house, how can I get him to help me in business." As a society, we've let the media tell us there is an impenetrable wall between the sexes. How do we let the perceived battle of the sexes enter into the confines of our most sacred relationship?

No one knows you like your spouse…sometimes she knows more about you than you know about yourself. That knowledge comes from many years of being with you. And if you entered into this sacrament under the right circumstances, no one on earth loves you more than your spouse. You know that you have each others back and many times it's just you two against the world.

We decided before I left the corporate world, that in order to fully dedicate my time to the family business, we had to build the framework of a good business relationship within our marriage. So we took a marital retreat for deep introspection and we committed to read a book by Michael Gerber called "The E-Myth". The book was the turning point in how we ran all of our businesses and the quiet introspection gave us clarity in how we would work together. So we took on this retreat by locking ourselves in a hotel room over a weekend to get this done. Here are the building blocks that came from that retreat.

Be Honest About Your Fears

We did an exercise that was paramount to our success in business and it started with two questions: *1.What is your biggest fear about going into business with your spouse? 2. What are her/his strengths that will make us successful?* We started this with one rule in mind:

Be honest, with loving tact, because this is your God given partner and it is required.

Ten years after that retreat, we reviewed some documents from that meeting and were amazed by our written responses. It's wild to see how far we've come in thoughts and action in order to get to where we are today. The issues that appeared in our marriage at that time surfaced as we contemplated this business venture.

Pop's Response: My biggest fears are:
  1) Make business decisions w/ total disregard to the financial impact.
  2) Lead with your heart and not your head.
  3) You will not pay attention to vital details.
  4) Dream too big too quickly.
  5) Your manner of handling money.
Rita's Strengths are:
  6) Vision of what she wants.
  7) Never gives up (pit-bull).
  8) Rapport builder and relationship artist.

Mom's Response: My biggest fears are:
  1) Tight with money; not willing to invest to grow.
  2) Not trusting my judgment.
  3) Questioning every decision I make
Will's Strengths are:
  4) Handling money
  5) Negotiation w/ vendors
  6) Creating business systems & measurements

This exercise will help you put everything on the table that may have concerned you in the past. The advantage that we have is that we've been in business ventures together prior to this exercise. So we had a track record that we could refer to. But for those of you where this will be your first business venture; look at the way you handle household decisions as a barometer.

Business Roles Should Leverage Strengths

I remember in graduate school using an instrument called the Myers-Briggs Instrument to determine how we made decisions. The instrument could tell if you relied more on logic or feeling or were you an introvert or an extrovert? And if you understood how you made decision then you could rely on that method of decision making as your strength. Supposedly, many things go into how you make decisions and this tool could distill it down for you. Well, it wasn't perfect because I got a different evaluation every time I took it. The point I'm trying to make is that our strengths and weaknesses must be clear as we decide what roles we will take in this business. And your roles will have either a positive or negative impact on the business' success.

First, let me broach the subject of leadership (who is the boss?) and how it may stir up many unexpected feelings. Rita & I are both Christians and were raised in the Catholic Church and our marriage is based on those values. The husband is the spiritual lead in the family and the wife is "the helper"; equal partner made from the rib of Adam. This is our faith and we began our marriage with this premise but soon the real world slithered in and tested our faith.

We are both very aggressive in what we want and we're determined to get it. Let me just say that there were many "clash of the titans" in our home on many issues as big as selecting the house to live in to something as small as how to properly load the dishwasher. The desire to compete brings out the need to win and it can get ugly. To run a business successfully, you must do your best to leave traditional home roles at home.

Now, let's get back to strengths. In business there are key roles that every organization must designate in order for the operations to run efficiently. They are:

1. *Executive Leadership – President*
2. *Finance – VP of Finance, Treasurer, Controller*
3. *Operations – VP of Ops, Office Mgr., Payroll, HR*
4. *Sales & Marketing – Sales Mgr., Mkt. Mgr.*

You may find yourself wearing multiple hats in the beginning and later delegating to employees as you grow. This may allow you to move toward areas of the business that excites you more. We looked closely at ourselves and wrote down our fears and strengths and then we assigned roles in the business based on that data.

Organization Chart:

- <u>*President-Rita*</u>: *Visionary. Ability to drive us to complete the mission.*
- <u>*Treasurer-Will*</u>: *Detailed on money issues. Understands cash flow.*
- <u>*Operations-Rita*</u>: *Trained in designing systems and how each job function pertains to achieving the mission.*
- <u>*Sales & Marketing-Will*</u>: *Trained in developing sales teams and implementing marketing strategies.*

We now knew what are responsibilities were but what would happen if we disagreed? What a novel thought since we never disagree – funny. We've come to many stalemates in our marriage and occasionally would resort to dirty tactics to get our way; leaving the other feeling invalidated and manipulated. Not good. We made a promise to play fair and abide by our rules.

You must promise to bring the integrity & honesty of your marriage into your business

---

Before we started this new business we felt we needed to go to a boot camp for our marriage. A business venture can be tough on a relationship so we needed to develop a Kevlar vest around our marriage to protect it. So we attended a Christian seminar called "I Still Do".

This weekend seminar is designed to rekindle the meaning of your marriage and commitment to each other. I can say without a shadow of a doubt; it did just that for us. I saw my wife with new eyes and a re-opened heart. We were so much better for this weekend and we wanted the same commitment (covenant) in our business relationship. I knew that I had chosen the best partner as my wife and the mother of our children, but now I can feel the same way in business. Reluctance became excitement and anticipation.

The weekend also confirmed to us that we would never, under any circumstance, break our promises to each other. Though we never broke our marriage vow of fidelity, we were both guilty of not putting God, and the other, first in everything we did. This was a compromise to what we held most dear. Potential compromises of integrity were not just a threat to us, but we feel it is threat to our American way of life. Just as some have lost their honesty and integrity in their marriage; we have as a nation lost it in our business dealings.

There is too much mounting evidence that the problems in marriage and business all stem from broken promises. We have become a nation of "promise until it becomes inconvenient" type of people. And if we endeavor, as married business owners, to do great things and make an impact in business, we must renew the covenant of integrity in all we do moving forward.

Why do we mention broken promises in this book? Just look at the disintegration of integrity in our society. If you look back in history to the early days of our country; a man's word was his bond and his name was sacred. If a merchant gave his word to another regarding the delivery of his product or service; you could count on it. It was as good as gold. "It will be on your dock by Tuesday 9am" meant only one thing; it would be there by Tuesday 9am.

In those days, an agreement and a handshake between business people was all that was needed to cement a transaction. And if it had to be written to note the details, this was normally done on one sheet of paper to keep it simple. Today because of our society's proclivity to be dishonest, contract paperwork has grown to ten, twenty, thirty plus sheets with hundreds of clauses sometimes to protect, yet often to confuse.

And back then, people revered the leaders of our country. It was believed that those in leadership positions were above reproach because of their commitment. And did they commit. Some gave everything they had for this country to separate from England. Most sacrificed their wealth, land and homes. Many were considered fugitives and were constantly running from English armed forces. And too many paid for the freedoms we enjoy today with their lives. Our early citizens of this great land had great faith in their leaders because our leaders had great integrity. Fast forward to today and we have some politicians who regularly practice dishonesty. And their first impulse is to lie if they are caught doing something unscrupulous. And they only tell the truth if they have no other recourse.

These people seek political office to be served; not to serve. And I'm not talking about all politicians; just the ones whose non-pious activities cast a negative light on the whole group. This small minority of politicians look for ways to benefit themselves while all the time lying to the public.

Then there is that group of business people who chose to be dishonest in order to profit. There's no rule in business that says you must lie and cheat to be profitable. The rule is: *If you serve your customer and community with a good product or service, that public will reward you with great profits.* Leaders of companies like AIG, Enron and MCI have robbed the public trust and money to line their own pockets.

My parent's would say that you should never make a promise you cannot keep, so always keep your promises. It seems that they maybe the last generation that believed in maintaining bonds built through promises. They believed that your word meant something and if you didn't keep it, well you would be ostracized by your friends and others in the community.

Today, we are not living up to the values of integrity that we were taught. We have become a society of convenience and we give our sense of character away at a whim. Instead of "delivery on Tuesday" it became "I could get it there mid-week". And instead of "delivery by 9am" it became "delivery sometime early morning or late afternoon". Rita and I can spot the people who have tossed their integrity in the trash by the types of commitments they make to us. We hear things like "I will be at your office around 9ish" or "We will try to make that deadline". We call it the **"Try-ish Syndrome"** and when we hear this in our business dealings we are immediately put on guard.

Its not that we don't do business with people like this, it's just that we anticipate problems and develop alternative plans so that we can keep our commitments. Then there are those times where we are pleasantly surprised by the business people who under commit yet over deliver. I say just do what you say you are going to do and abandon that tactic because it doesn't help your credibility. In order to be successful in marriage and business, you must have a rebirth of integrity in your new covenant.

So based on this, we decided to make a **new covenant** with each other in business just as sacred as our marital vows. We stood before God over 20 years ago and made a commitment to each other. We promised that nothing would come between our love and care for each other. That meant not a person, sickness or poverty and surely not a business venture. Here was our covenant:

Our Business Covenant
Marriage before Business

And I vow to you that.
1. *The business will mirror our values to the world; the world will not dictate our business values.*
2. *I will be in the business with my spouse; but the business will not be in my marriage.*
3. *If our union is ever in jeopardy due to the business, we will exit the business in a timely manner.*

It's so easy to let bickering and guilt in business activities crawl into your bed at night. The bed is sacred to the marriage and nothing else belongs there; especially your business. Your business must be a reflection of your marriage to the world, so if your marriage is not solid your business will not be solid. Your customers and employees will be able to see the hypocrisy and will not follow your lead. And it may manifest itself in lost customers, lower sales, low employee morale and even the exit of vital staff.

Accomplish the Business Mission

Now that your covenant is renewed, you are now able embrace the reality that you are running a business and you need to treat it as such. Remember that you are in business with a partner that you love more than life and your partner deserves your utmost respect in all dealings. But…you are still running a business with roles, objectives and responsibilities.

Once you've determined your strengths and your roles in the business then you must honor those positions. If you've agreed to the roles and responsibilities of those positions then it is incumbent upon you to do the tasks assigned. For me that wasn't the difficult part. My problem was with how important decisions were made, especially, when I disagreed with the decision being made by someone other than me.

Okay, I'm showing that my ego has been bruised a few times, yet I can almost guarantee that the same will happen to you and your spouse. Traditional roles in the family maybe turned upside down on a business decision. When we decided on our respective roles we were just fine as we grew this venture. Decisions were made based on the job description and we did our jobs and moved forward. Until one day when I felt emasculated by my wife…the bruised ego.

We decided that I would be president of our real estate company and she would be president of the Montessori schools with all the rights bestowed to that position (for the sake of this book we are concentrating on the schools only). I was the treasurer for the Montessori schools and she would yield to my recommendation on every financial issue. She did this because she trusted me and she let me do my job. Yet, there were issues that we both felt passionately about and our viewpoints were opposed. What a unique problem ah…married people disagreeing.

As president, she could trump my decision when she felt it was for the betterment of the business. Someone has to make the final decision on all stalemates and that person was her. One day, there was an opportunity that would give us another revenue stream and a decision had to be made. We talked about it for many days and we couldn't come to common ground. A decision had to be made soon in order to get people and resources moving on this project.

Suffice it to say, she made the decision I was opposed to. And that thing I promised would not get into our bed; it was smack dap in the middle of our California king size. My resentment became obvious and she wanted to talk about what was wrong. So I spilled the beans as was required by our commitment to each other. Now she was hurt and there were two people who love each other hurt by each other.

What about the covenant we both agreed to? We hugged each other and reminded ourselves that the marriage was more important than anything else. We were both ready to yield to the wishes of the other in order to keep the marriage on track…damn the business.

But that wasn't what we agreed to when we started this and I was in violation of our agreement. I asked her not to retract the presidential decision she made and we moved in that initial direction.

This will happen to you to some degree as it unfolded for us and you must have a strategy to defeat this enemy in your marriage and business. Rita developed a method of holding hands throughout an argument so that we don't lose touch with each other. There were disagreements where I probably squeezed her hand harder than I should of but she remained committed to the process; committed to us. It's amazing how hard it is to stay mad at her when we touch each other. We then fall back on our trust in each other; we are back on track.

Mom & Pop's Key Points:

1. Your marriage must survive; the business is always secondary.
2. Leverage your strengths for the business and always treat your spouse like a loving partner; not a business partner.
3. Play fair and honor the rules you've designate for marriage/business.

Mom & Pop's To Do's:

4. Take a marital retreat with your spouse to renew your bond and set the stage for your business roles. We recommend an event sponsored by Family Life called *"Weekend to Remember"*.
5. If you need counseling; seek it and heed their advice. A good counselor is just another coach.
6. Put together a business plan for your new venture. We've used *"Business Plan Pro"* from Palo Alto Software.
7. Develop your own Marriage/Business Covenant to keep you on track when you hit bumps in the road. Take your time and keep talking about it until it can be etched in stone.

CLARITY OF WHY

I'm going to make a few assumptions as we go through this process together. First, I will assume that you are already accomplished in your career of choice. And that you've had a decent level of career success but you know there is something more to this life. Second, is that you are looking to make a change… a change from the world of an employee to the world of an entrepreneur. There are thousands of career paths and they eventually lead to the same fork in the road: lifetime employee or business owner. And we've deduced that you've purchased this book because you've made the wonderful decision to take the road to freedom and financial independence.

It is not money that will lead you to freedom and financial independence but a change in your thought-set. Getting rid of your PWL and developing a whole new thought-set that will serve you moving forward. This group of self-serving affirming thoughts will remain in the forefront of your mind when confronted with negativity; internal and external. The enemy within will find many reasons for you not to take this new path of prosperity and this battle will be an ongoing process until you new thought-set has taken root. This will take time and consistency.

Now, let's address the enemy in the outside world and how it will come from a multitude of areas. It may show itself in that well meaning family member or friend who doesn't want you to get hurt or fail in this process. Well meaning hearts want to show you how great things are currently and trying something new will never equal the level of success you have at this moment. Do your best to avoid conversations with these people. You don't want to take guidance from a person who has never blazed the trail you are seeking.

Be very wary of the friend or family member who maybe a little more covert in their attempt to have you stray from this path. Conversations may sound supportive but are tainted with envy and jealousy. They fear you will break away from them on your move toward success. I sound paranoid but I believe that I'm just a good read of people. Nevertheless, I read somewhere that Donald Trump's paranoia is what keeps him motivated to succeed in all his business dealings. We had friends, another couple, who later admitted to us that they once felt this way.

When we bought our first commercial building, they invited us out to dinner to celebrate our first move to exit the daily grind of a job. It was great that they thought enough of us to go out of their way to acknowledge this milestone in our lives. But toward the end of the evening as we were walking to the parking lot, the wife said to Rita, "Don't you feel that this puts too much pressure on Will because if this fails, he will have to pay two mortgages?" At that time, I was the only one bringing in an income.

Rita kept walking but I could feel each one of her steps become heavier as she walked toward the car. But, in usual Rita fashion, she made me so proud with her response and it turn out to be another affirmation that I had the world's best wife and business partner. She said "I appreciate your concern for us, but we've done our due diligence and we are boldly stepping forward into our future. And this deal will do just the opposite of what you suggest, it will take pressure off Will's shoulders and the building will pay for itself and our home mortgage as well".

We did our homework to drastically reduce the downside of this deal and we were not going to let the world get in our way. As we grew from real estate to other businesses these friends lost touch with us. Many attempts to invite them out were never met with a reply. We lost touch and realized that our new lives had dug a huge chasm between us and it broke our hearts. It became clear that friendships are based on mutual interests and activities and they no longer felt we had much in common. You may experience similar casualties on your trek from employee to entrepreneur. This journey is more rewarding when you surround yourself with like-minded individuals.

All this was mentioned in this book to bring clarity to why. The reason to make this transformation has to be bigger than anything that has ever motivated you in the past. As my friend Bob puts it, *"The reason to do this has to be much bigger than you, because there will come a time that this reason will be the only thing left in you to propel you forward when you feel there is nothing left to give and all hope is gone."* Sounds a little melodramatic, but every entrepreneur reaches a point where he second guesses the business idea; the dream and eventually themselves. This is the main reason that the "why" is so important.

His wise words have shown its truth in every step of my business life. This path will challenge your thought-set, your relationships, your finances and your sense of self. This is why the reason "why" must be bigger than you. But through these challenges comes the rewards of freedom and financial independence. It will open up a whole new world which is a 180° turn from your current way of thinking. Please do not take this phase lightly because it's easy to dismiss this as simplistic. I know you've heard it or read it a million times before. But your "why" will determine your level of success.

Bob has given me many nuggets of wisdom as I started my transition. Bob is a millionaire who started and sold many businesses in his lifetime. And though we come from completely different worlds, not to mention a 20 year age gap, we both have a love of fly fishing which brought us together. On a brief trip to the Florida Keys to attempt to catch a tarpon on a fly line (fly fishing stuff), I informed him that I had to cut the trip short to go back to Cleveland to dismiss a sales rep and close a huge deal in his place by end of business tomorrow. This was a normal occurrence for me in the software business, but still a major pain in the _ _ _!

I told Bob that I couldn't wait to get out of the rat race and engulf myself in the business with my wife. He pretended not to understand why I would want to leave such a lucrative career in such haste. This was his typical coy manner when he was about to put on his coaching hat. "Will, you are making great money running your team, right? There are always problems on the path to success and leaving will not eliminate problems", Bob would say. "I'm tired of these problems, so maybe I'm ready for a new set of problems" was my reply.

He always said that I had to be ready for this new set of problems because these challenges will be drastically different than anything that I had to endure before. "If you are trying to build a franchise-model business, you are in for a new set of problems…..as a matter of fact, a new set of everything." He said with a theatric flare because…that was just his way of getting his point across. As we stood on the deck of this small boat in the Gulf of Mexico trying to find a school of tarpon swimming by, he wanted to impart some more wisdom.

He mentioned that my formal education process from elementary school to graduate school was designed to prepare me to be a good employee. As a business owner, he loved the education system because it allowed him to select only the best to run his company. A little training on his company's culture and process and the person was on her way to making his business more profitable. He made the comparison of our education system to crawling/walking /running.

Elementary school through high school is an education that's synonymous with crawling. "In these years, you learn just enough to move forward so as not to be a burden to society". You learn to do things to make enough money to survive and that is it. These are the people making minimum wage because they offer minimum value to a business owner. This is the longest and slowest path to wealth, so just like crawling you will not get anywhere fast.

College is where you learn to walk in the parlance of making money. "In college, you prove to your professor that you can learn (meaning take information in and spit it back out on written tests) and that is all you do; nothing else of any significant value to an employer". You haven't mastered any discernable skills to make money work for you, but like walking you can start moving in the right direction on your own. And then your first job and or graduate school is like running.

"Here you learn how business works and may begin to master some discernable skills to help a company reach its goals. It's like running because you can quickly offer value that can be measured on a frequent basis." To make your company goals on a consistent basis means that you must have mastered a skill and have a clear direction to success. Just like the sprinter who has mastered the skills necessary to win in running the 100 meter dash, you are able to run fast to a clearly defined goal with a financial prize waiting for you at the finish line.

"Now that you've spent your entire life learning how to crawl/walk/run in preparation for a job in the business world, entrepreneurship flips that all around by demanding that you do this on your hands", Bob said with a chuckle. "You must learn how to walk and run on your hands to be successful, or at least that is the way it will feel at first". And one of the major reasons for this is that our schooling never prepared us with a financial, leadership and visionary education. Every entrepreneur must receive their life degree in this coursework sooner or later. And I prefer sooner.

In essence, great entrepreneurial leaders see the world differently than employees. Some employees don't understand the need to measure certain areas of the business and how it impacts other areas. When I was an employee, I too looked at some of those things as a waste of time and effort. But as you figuratively walk on your hands as a leader; you can't help but see things differently from that vantage point. You begin to notice how every aspect of the business fits together to create an integrated system of success. You gain a better understanding as to the role your customers and investors play in your business. Your vision becomes so clear that you can see the possibilities beyond the four walls of your company.

And as one makes this transition, it can be an awkward feeling because this is a major departure from your years of schooling. Even if you've been in a managerial position, it hasn't sharpened the periphery vision necessary to be a great entrepreneur. I can say with a considerable amount of certainty that none of us have received a formal education in entrepreneurship. And even fewer of us have received a functional financial education. Courage to start your business isn't enough; it takes a different kind of training.

Here was his lesson: The same skills I learned to be a great employee may not serve me as I become a great entrepreneur. He wanted to make it emphatically clear that a self-employed person is not an entrepreneur. A self-employed person is a person who doesn't make money for his company unless he is doing the work. And an entrepreneur makes money when he isn't even there….even when he is fly-fishing. In your zest and zeal to run toward making a living in your own business you should run from being self-employed with just as much speed.

We went to lunch after I packed my belongings to catch the next flight home. We caught some grouper (this is a type of fish) and we took it to our favorite restaurant to have prepared to our desire. Sitting on the outside deck of this restaurant with the sea breeze on our faces, Bob felt the need to continue his lesson. "In all my years of business I've conclude that there are two areas of thought that make entrepreneurs different from employees", Bob said. There maybe more than these two but in all of his conversations with both types of people he could distill it down to this:

Employee's Mentality	vs	**Entrepreneur's Mentality**
Entitlements	vs	Value
Security	vs	Freedom

Entitlement is a *"what is in it for me"* mentality. Now, don't get mad at us when we talk about entitlements because this is a mental defect of most Americans. This condition was brought upon our society as early as "The New Deal" of President Franklin D. Roosevelt (FDR) administration. He formed the early beginnings of today's Social Security system at a time when our country was coming off a devastating depression. But today, the costs have gotten out of hand and we can no longer meet our obligation to the retirees without running up a huge deficit.

This program could be sustainable even today if our government would of use the true "lock-box" method and kept their hands off those funds. But history has shown us that the federal government can't resist spending money they have….and even money they don't have. But is it an entitlement if we paid into it? My answer is no. The problem is that each citizen takes more money from it than they put in and as generations go by. This is because our cost of living keeps going up from inflation created by the Federal Reserve. If the cycle continues the system will not sustain itself.

Please remember that our government gave us the impression that Social Security was an investment in our future retirement but here is the problem. You can only receive a return on an investment when you create a product or service as in the business world. Our government never created anything. They just collect taxes, make false promises and redistribute the dollars from one person to the next in order to solidify votes.

So the genesis of this entitlement mentality started with FDR and continued with Lyndon B. Johnson (LBJ) in the 1960's with the Medicare/Medicaid system. And during those two eras the labor unions, through collective bargaining and other tools, furthered this way of thinking into the 21st century. Now, I know we are treading on sensitive territory here but we are attempting to expose the reason for this way of thinking.

The entitlement mentality may be the sole culprit in removing the desire for some employees to have pride in their performance. We've have heard many employees say "It's just a job" in a manner that shows no personal ownership in something they maybe doing for eight hours a day. Merit pay, which is compensation based on performance, has been replaced with cost of living increases and tenure. And there are some government workers who don't contribute a single penny to their retirement/pension funds; it's paid by the taxpayer. And that same taxpayer in the private sector must contribute to their on retirement without any assistance.

I'm not angry at these employees who have these benefits and are fighting like-the-dickens to keep them. But some would say it is unfair and unsustainable in today's economic environment. Some companies and government officials agreed to these terms in negotiations with unions when times were good. But after the 2008 crash, we were surprised to find that the good times were over and the bill became due. States like Ohio, Wisconsin & California are finding it hard to pay that bill and companies like GM & Chrysler have found it so hard that they needed a federal bailout.

As for entrepreneurs, they don't seek entitlements but look to deliver value in order to gain. They know that if they deliver a product or service that offers value to the consumer, they will be successful. They know that to the degree they serve their customers with value, to that same degree that customer will serve them with value (higher sales and net earnings). In the same breath; they know that if they fail in their mission to deliver value, their business could meet a swift demise. Sorry, but there is no government bailout for him so he must find ways to move forward and be successful. No company or government funded pension plan or medical plan here either. Only the confidence that he will build a business that will grow in value for years to come.

Then there is security and stability. Most of us went to school and chose our careers in an effort to find security and stability. My dad found this when he started working as a laborer for Chrysler on the day of my birth and retired 34 years to the date. Those types of jobs are no longer available, but most are still striving for them. What most fail to realize is these types of jobs are very hard to find, if not impossible.

What is most sad about these people is that in an effort to find security and stability they are willing to stay in a job they don't like, maybe even hate. This activity, or inactivity, will slowly suck the life out of that person. Over time his morale goes down, as well as his health. And so does the quality of the products or service he was hired to deliver.

This hurts the employer by putting the company in jeopardy of losing business, yet the employer is still paying them to slowly kill the business. Eventually the person is fired or decides to move on, but during this dance no one wins. In an effort to find this mythical security and stability, they have forgotten the power they have to find joyous work and to be fulfilled in life.

The entrepreneur is motivated by something significantly different: freedom. The freedoms to create, allocate time and resources, delegate and vacate. They know that there is a cost to freedom and they are willing to pay it. During the times of slavery, African Americans knew the cost of freedom if they decided to pursue it. They'd be chased by dogs, whipped, have their toes removes so they couldn't run and even death.

Knowing the cost some still pursued freedom. Not all slaves decided to take the Underground Railroad just like many employees will decide not to take the path of entrepreneurship. Those slaves who decided to remain on the plantation chose stability & security because they had shelter, food and clothing but freedom was worth more to those who escaped.

To get to the "why" we must be open to the fact that we need a change our thought-set. We have to understand all the negative influences, including our family and friends, and their impact on that process. As you ask yourself these tough questions you may find that you have more clarity than before. And clarity is so important on this long and rewarding journey.

Mom & Pop's Key Points:

1. Your "why" must be big enough to get you through the moments of uncertainty, hesitation and doubt.
2. Start your business seeking freedom and drive your business delivering value to your customers & employees.
3. Entrepreneurs think differently. <u>Embrace the change</u>.

Mom & Pop's To Do's:

4. Take time to meditate (pray) on your "why" till it is clear. Make bedtime sacred in discussing issues with each other.
5. Read books (audio too) that teach you how to live in the now. Knowing how to live in the now will give you clarity of why.
6. Read "Excuses Be Gone" by Dr. Wayne W. Dyer to help you knock down walls to your marital & business success.

CLARITY OF WHAT

Now that we have a good sense of why to start a new life as business owners, we still have to decide what the hell to do in business. Most of us make the decision of what to do long before we have convinced ourselves as to why. These people normally hit bumps in the road early in the process and then give up on the idea all together. They close up shop faster than the time it took to open. Their level of commitment invested was so low that they thought it better to just cut bait and run.

They then say things like "you can't make enough money doing this" or "it's a major headache running your own business" or "it just took too much time". All of which are said to validate their decision to not move forward. I've seen the faces of these people after they've closed their doors. I've seen the defeat in their eyes and I've heard the sound of desperation in their voices. For the most part, you can eliminate a fast and early exit of your business if you take the time to understand your why. As my coach Bob would say: *"Your reason to do this has to be bigger and more inspiring than all the reasons not to"*.

So, let's get to the fun part of deciding what you want to do. I know….you know what you want to do and you've already planned it out in your mind. This is a very normal start because we all begin this way. But let me give you some data that may spare you some time, money and heartache. Rita & I have had the chance to talk to nearly 30 entrepreneurs (mostly couples) and many have open their kimonos to share their most important and sensitive lessons. These lessons aren't infallible like biblical parables written on ancient scrolls. But they are critical lessons from the battles of business and they may help you decide your "what".

Rule #1
Do not make your current profession your new line of business.

I can hear it now, *Aw man that was what I was going to do!* We have seen this screenplay so many times because every single couple that we have masterminded with has started this way. To be perfectly honest; we started our first consulting business in this same fashion. But like all lessons in life; your learning is only completed through experience. We were told by others, and in books we read, that we should not start off like this but like a child; you never believe that fire is hot until you touch it.

We began our careers in the technology business: computer hardware & software. After many years of success, we decided to start our own consulting company. I would leverage my company contacts and customers and Rita would put together a team to write business applications.

Rita had been trained in programming and project management, so she was responsible for building the application for our clients. Occasionally, she would bring on a contract programmer to help complete a task in a timely manner. But in essence it was just Rita in a room generating software code. She also did the project management which entailed meeting with the clients, determining milestones and stuff like that.

Okay, I will move forward to show you the lesson that we learned here. Rita left a job as a project manager because she was working 60 hours a week making her boss rich. Only to find herself in our new company, working 75+ hours a week making herself crazy. She could never take time away to find new clients because she was too busy doing all the work. And when she did have time to find new clients that meant she wasn't working on a project; which meant she wasn't making money. In consulting, those times you don't have a client engagement was called sitting on the beach, but it wasn't anything like a beach.

We chose a business where she could leverage her expertise but in the analogy of using a lever; she was the fulcrum taking all the pressure. She didn't have time to do anything but work and became disenchanted rather quickly. I was still managing my sales team at my job and could only assist in bringing on clients in my spare time. But my spare time was shrinking fast due to my large quota commitment. My poor wife felt alone with no one to lean on.

We recommend that you not choose a business that leverages your job expertise because it quickly becomes just another job. I know this sounds counterintuitive, but remember that you decided to start a business so that you could have more time, more money and more freedom. This situation will not get you any of those things. When we brought on a contractor to help out, Rita found herself redoing some of his work because it didn't match up to the standards of our company or the client. This was because Rita didn't have time to properly train him or allow him time for a learning curve. Rita said to me, "I feel that my work is better than his so I have to make it right". This is a major shortcoming of the perfectionist professional running a business in his area of expertise.

She felt the only one who could produce work that the customer would like was her. I can recall a conversation one evening where I urged her to find more competent help to get the projects done and she ended our conversation by yelling, "These projects would never be successful without me doing them"! And as she made her proud exit from the room; she quickly returned within a few minutes to seek my forgiveness. She held me and said, "How can I ever grow this business when every customer interaction relies on me?" She was in distress over this.

In our mastermind groups, we've met doctors, lawyers and dentist in the same situation. They believe that they have a business but cash doesn't flow in the door unless they do the work. They are the ones who have to get in every morning and do the job until the end of the day. They don't have a business they have a job.

Now here is where we make a purposeful pause in the book. It's okay if you decide you want to start a company where you are the company, where you must be the one "doing it" day in and day out in order to make money. It's your choice if you take this path because there is an excellent chance that you could make a lot of money if your skill set is in demand. It's incumbent upon us to make you aware of the pitfalls and the great potential that lies before you. If this is what you want then stop here and go to the next chapter. If you desire freedom coupled with your dream of owning a business, please move forward to the next rule.

Rule #2
Work to build a business based on a franchise model (sound business system)

No matter what line of business you choose to create as an entrepreneur it will ultimately end as being one of two things: a self-employed business or a franchise model business. Starting a self-employed business is very hard to stop once you start. I compare it to that carousel in the elementary school playground. You grab the steel bar and then you start to run; pushing as hard as you can to get some speed.

You invite others to get on with you (customers) and their weight makes the job harder so you have to push harder to keep up the speed (demanding more of your time, energy & expertise). You are working so hard pushing your carousel called a business. You cannot slow it down because your customers are demanding more and you are paralyzed in motion; afraid to let go. By now the carousel has picked up so much speed that if you let go you may injure the business. Or should I say injure yourself because you are the business.

You are caught in the syndrome of doing it and doing it and you just can't get off. Then it sets in; the worry that if you take a break that the business will dry up and go away. Desire to branch out and be your own boss has turned into a fear that you can't keep up this pace. Your nerves are being tested with the feeling that you are reaching a breaking point and you have to make a change. Ironically this is the same feeling that propelled you to leave your corporate job in the first place; now its back. How could you allow this to happen again?

There is another business model that we recommend you thoroughly investigate: the franchise model. Building a business on a franchise model will free you from the day-to-day grind of your business and allow you to do those things that add value and excitement to your life. Rita and I have the strong belief that our business should work for us and not us working for the business.

I would be fooling you if I said it started off that way. In the beginning we worked our butts off like any new business owners finding ourselves exhausted at the end of each day. The pivot point to our success was when we decided to make a 180° turn in how we ran the business. In Michael Gerber's books he drove home a concept that has made all the difference for us: *work on the business, not in the business*.

When we opened our Montessori Schools, we decided to put our newly found business knowledge into practice. This time we chose a business where neither of us had any expertise and we hired people to do the job so we didn't have to. But the most important thing we did was to build a business system. This is where we spent our time fleshing out everything done in the business. Our business systems were our methods of doing it day in and day out with all of our policies and procedures along with ways to measure our progress.

Measurements are key in order to get better because you must inspect what you expect. So we developed an executive dashboard that allowed us to take a daily peek into every aspect of our business to see how it was doing. We developed tolerance levels for each key area so when something was in the "green"; it was running properly. If it was in the "yellow"; it needed our attention and "red" was bad.

When you fully understand every process in your business and how it should function for maximum results, you have inadvertently built a system. In our business there was a system for everything we did: how to answer the phone, greet customers, clean a bathroom, etc. And once the system was documented, we constantly looked for ways to innovate; make each system better and more efficient than before.

Routinely, our staff would get together to review certain systems. Sometimes a system would be dismantled in order to ascertain how we could do it better. Our goal was always centered on cost effectiveness and customer satisfaction. And at times we would redefine what optimum meant and develop matrices to measure it. We discovered that even the best of staff needs to be measured against the goal and they normally looked forward to the feedback. These measurements helped them understand where they were and how to get back on track, if necessary.

Developing and innovating business systems are vital actions for your business. It frees up your time to do other important things. There are tasks in every business that are either tactical or strategic and as a business owner you must select those that grow the business. No more hours fixing toilets and light fixtures, as well as doing all the bookkeeping. Our systems allowed us to farm those activities out while we concentrated on things that grew the business.

Another value of developing a strong business system is it allows you to duplicate. In business there is a saying *"If the business is not expanding, then the business is contracting by default"*. So if you are not looking for ways to grow your brand and revenue then you should sell it immediately and just get out. Growth is the lifeblood of the business and your employees' future. Good employees will always want more opportunity and that cannot happen unless you are growing.

What we discovered is that after we hammered out the wrinkles in our business system, it was easier to open another facility. After doing our due diligence on demographics, psychographics and location, we simply used our system to open the new school. Our system had everything we needed from the architectural plans, construction management to training the staff on how to prepare lesson plans. Every system was documented in one huge repository.

How did we know it was a good system? Well, let's just say that it took 15 months for the first location to make a positive cash flow. But with the second school; we began cash flowing in less that five months. All of our experience went into the system with only the perfected lessons being applied. The litmus test for the system is that we not only duplicate our success, but we duplicated it faster.

Though will be discussing exit strategies later in the book, I want to touch on it briefly to show the value of a sound business system when selling a business. We know of two couples who sold their businesses in 2007. One couple had a medical practice and the other had a dental practice. In our mastermind meetings, we all agree to keep confidences in order to properly serve all members in moving toward our goals. And telling this story doesn't in anyway infringe upon that commitment.

The two married physicians had three offices throughout the city where they divided their time. They were the only doctors in the practice and only made money when they saw patients. They had minimal systems in place because they were in the mode of just "doing it" as the patients came along. Because of changes in medical insurance; they decided to sell their practice to pursue law enforcement and writing children's books.

When they sold their business they felt that they received a fair price from another group of physicians. They told us that they received a little more than what their annual salaries were at that time, plus some cash for the sale of some medical equipment. A twelve year practice was sold for what was a little more than their 2006 W-2s. We thought that was good but not good enough.

The dentist practice was a little different because it was built on a franchise model. They had four locations and a staff of 5 dentists, including themselves, to cover all locations. After eight years of practicing, they had an ever expanding patient list of families and friends. With their business system perfected, they had growth every year for four years straight. What made this most interesting was that this couple wasn't looking to sell their business. The buyer found them and pursued them vigorously for two years.

They sold it to a gentleman who had retired from the aerospace industry and made his money in real estate. He liked their business model because it could run without him being there and he didn't need to be a dentist. He bought the business and signed a 20 year NNN lease on their buildings.

Here is where the two deals are distinctly different. Because the dentists had a strong business system in place, they were able to demand a multiple of their net earnings to close the transaction. When the deal was completed, they received a check at closing that was 4.5 times their annual net earnings. I don't know the details of the financials, but I would venture to say that they were pleased with the outcome.

I hope this example shows you the value of a franchise model based on a sound business system. If you are going to build a business with an airtight business system, you can expect a large multiple of your net earnings when you exit. Receiving a multiple of earnings is not exclusive to the dentist situation because they were lucky. No, this is a normal outcome when selling a franchise model business where you are not the business. Take the time to think every system through until they are bulletproof.

Mom & Pop's Key Points:

1. There is nothing wrong with a self-employed business but the leverage of a franchise model is what will make you free.
2. Take the time to hammer out all the systems in your business and document them. Work with your spouse and your staff to continuously innovate all processes.
3. Thinking about your exit is not premature. Ask yourself what your business will look like when it has reached the finish line.

Mom & Pop's To Do's:

4. Study industry trends to decide what line of business you want to pursue. Find a growing industry that could be done better.
5. With business plan in hand, talk to local bankers about SBA loans. Money is available; you have to go out and get it.
6. Sign up with Service Corp. of Retired Executives to get free counseling and mentoring on your new business. (SCORE.org).
7. Consider reading Napoleon Hill's *"The Law of Success"*. It will give more clarity to your "what".

PROTECTION FROM THE "Ps"

After discovering your "why" and your "what" you have the foundation to start your business venture. But every bit of success that you grow can all be taken away without the right protection. There are piranhas in the waters of success and they have no conscience when it comes to taking it from you. You can't walk through this door simply hoping to make it to the other side untouched. This will be your family's livelihood and no one should take it away on a whim.

We live in interesting times where our government is spending like an insane profligate and our legal system will allow the most frivolous lawsuits to pass through their courts. In our legal system, even if your case is solid and you have the highest probability or winning, you will still incur substantial legal fees just to defend yourself. And our government, which was designed to serve the people, now expects us to serve them so they tax us beyond our means. At times it appears that everyone is looking for someone to fund their spending spree; and their eyes are on you.

It reminds me of a conversation we had with our accountant Diane Kennedy (author of "Tax Loopholes of the Rich). In one of our initial sessions we talked about growing the business as well as some accounting and legal issues we were facing at the time. After Rita asked her a certain question, she paused and took a deep breath and looked her square in the eye. And in a very direct tone she said "Be aware of the bull's eye on your back, be very aware". In essence, she was saying that our government, our customers, our employees and our family & friends can see it clearly and they maybe taking aim….be prepared.

At first, this seemed like pure paranoia and we thought we may have taken in a "doomsayer" as our accountant. But she was on target with that sentiment because it unfortunately played itself out in a few episodes on our journey through entrepreneurship. There maybe some people, for many different reasons, coming after you so that they can participate in your money as well. These entities that want to latch on to some of your success are what we call "The P Scoundrels". Their sole purpose is to take your wealth and you must develop a strategy to protect yourself. Let's take a look at them:

The P Scoundrels
- **Politicians** (Government)
- **Pirates** (Thieves of property/ideas/etc)
- **Patrons & Passersbys** (Customers & Employees)
- **Posterity** (Your children)
- **Phamily & Phriends** ("P" Family & Friends)

You may have noticed that I took some liberty in naming some scoundrels Phamily & Phriends because there is a distinction. These people are the polar opposite of loving family & friends who truly have your best interest at heart and celebrate your success. Envy & jealousy are not just human characteristics you find in people outside your circle but in people inside your circle. We will explain how to protect your wealth.

Phamily & Phriends Scoundrel Protection

When you become wealthy from your business, some of these P&Ps will come out of the woodwork to collect their share. Our disclaimer is that we are not cynical but just extremely cautious. 100% of all successful business people have already been pursued or will be pursued when it comes to their wealth. Lets say by now, your business has grown to the point that it throws off enough money that it can pay for a nicer home, car or vacation. In any circumstance, the whiff of your success is clearly within sniffing distance of this group of people.

Now it gets awkward because the P&Ps that you rarely speak to are coming to share in your success. Some are overt and some are covert; anyway you see them coming or feel them breathing down your neck. Some need genuine help and some are looking for easy money and you have to make the distinction between the two.

Real family and friends are proud to see you succeed and they pat you on the back and praise you. They even brag about you to people they know. They rarely ask for anything and because of that you are willing to share. This is the true definition of family & friends.

Don't misconstrue my tone as being stingy or greedy because our position is just the opposite. Money cannot grow by hoarding; it must flow freely in order to increase its flow. The river of cash becomes wider when we remove all obstacles to its flow. But we must be good stewards and not misuse this vital resource.

Now, let us address why we say the P&Ps are different. They don't stay in touch; they are envious of your success and back-bite often. They truly exemplify the crabs-in-the-box behavior. As soon as one looks as though they will climb out of the box to escape another one is below to pull him back down. These people don't have a place in your life and you would do well to eliminate them from your orbit.

For every part of your life you must have a protection strategy and it's your responsibility to use it! It's senseless to map out the strategy and then hesitate to use it. Money, your money, is a very sensitive subject and you must keep in mind that giving money to people you know will never teach them about money. So if you give someone money, the likelihood is very high that sooner or later they will be back for more.

Let me share with you our strategy for protection when it comes to P&Ps. First, we made the decision that without surrender, we will be on good terms with everyone we deem as P&Ps. It doesn't serve us to have ill-will toward anyone and it tends to only feed the flames of jealousy and animosity.

Secondly, we tell all that we don't give or lend money to Phamily & Phriends without the guidance of our financial advisor. In 2007, a P&P of my wife heard about a vacation we took and decided to make a drop in visit on us. We had not seen him in quite sometime because he thought that we changed since we became business owners. I personally felt an artic breeze in the times we had a chance to see each other.

He explained that he needed a little help to pay his two car notes and would be back on his feet in a couple of months and would pay us back. We gave him our advisors card and told him that it must be blessed by him before we are able to help out. We tell everyone who asks for a loan or gift that it would be insanity to pay an advisor and not heed his advice. Therefore, we don't make financial decisions without our advisor.

Here is the interesting part. He contacted the advisor and received explanation of the process; the loan documents, interest rate, collateral, etc. He was upset that this was no different than going to a bank; so he decided not to proceed. He was clearly looking for a handout and once that money was gone, he would be looking for another. We offered other avenues to help him (second job as handyman), but he declined them.

You must agree in your marriage on how to handle these types of people no matter which side of the family. Treat them all the same and follow through on your strategy every time. This consistency will reduce hostility during the holidays.

Politician Scoundrel Protection

The biggest expenses you will have in life are taxes and inflation (better known as the stealth tax). If the government can't take your money through inflation (debasing the dollar), then they will take it in taxes. And you can best believe that they will use these tools every chance they get to fund their projects and get votes. Believe it or not; there is a protection strategy from the government and these strategies are used by the richest people in America and you can learn them too.

As an employee, you have very little power to affect the amount of taxes you pay. You may think that through itemization of things like charity, real estate taxes, mortgage interest and alike that you are winning; you are not. Through the payroll tax code, a person making over $75k a year is paying more than 35% in taxes to federal, state, local government. Now throw in sales tax on items you must buy like clothing, some foods and gasoline. And add the tax (fees) you pay on things like driver's licenses, car tags, road tolls, etc. Now you may be paying more than 50% of your salary to the government.

But what's so insidious is that you work so hard for your money and yet you, are the one paid last. You see, Uncle Sam takes his share of your money first and throws to you whatever is left. We're not saying that taxes are bad because it takes tax money to keep our country moving. What I do have a problem with is how much we pay and how it is being used to serve the citizens. As for how it's being used; well that is a political subject that we will not touch within the bounds of this book. But how much you pay in taxes.....well we can address that.

To protect yourself against the Politician Scoundrels you must use the correct corporate entity. Using a sole-proprietorship or a partnership will put you into a bigger tax trap. When you start your business within the right entity you can get tremendous tax advantages that will allow you to control more of your money. We are not accountants but we have had a few good ones on our team and they've made such a big difference in what we pay in taxes. They've taught us to understand the tax ramification of any business deal we decide to pursue.

When you unlock the true power of a business, in the right entity, you can do just the opposite of what you did as an employee. As an employee, you pay your taxes first and operated your family budget on what remains. As a business, your daily operations are paid for by the revenue earned and whatever is remaining is then taxed. Now these are legitimate business expenses that are paid for by the business, but as the owner you may receive the benefit (please consult a qualified CPA). If done properly, you can owe the federal government nearly zero in federal taxes. This is a true statement just ask Warren Buffett. That means you could have your cars, health benefits, travel, cell phones and other expenses paid for within the confines of the business.

When we setup our first corporation, we asked ourselves a few important questions:

1) *What type of business are we operating in this entity?*
2) *How will this entity limit my tax exposure?*
3) *What types of assets do we want in this entity?*
4) *And when its time to exit the business, how will this entity allow us to get our value out of the business with the lowest tax?*

These are some important questions that must be answered with the guidance of a CPA and lawyer. Their experiences in these areas are invaluable because you want to reduce your legal and tax exposure as your business grows.

We decided to run each school and commercial property through its own individual LLC. This gave us the tax advantages of a corporation without the double taxation that came along with a "C" corporation. Under the strict guidance of our accountant, we could expense a large portion of the costs associated with travel for board meetings, etc. Our cars and cell phones were used in conducting our business, so a majority of those expenses were eligible (lease, gas, insurance, maintenance, etc.) Our healthcare costs were benefits to ownership, so they too were expensed. And there are so many more examples.

We paid ourselves a very small salary to lower our income tax bracket. Then our real estate companies would receive rents that would come to us as passive income, which is taxed at a lower rate than earned income. This again lowered our tax burden to the Politician Scoundrels.

We are just touching on some of the highlights of a protection strategy. We are not recommending that you use any of these strategies that we have outlined. The best strategy for you will be tailored to your situation by qualified personnel. The point we are trying to drive home is that you can substantially lower your tax burden and keep most of your money to be used to your benefit.

Pirate Scoundrel Protection

Imitation is the greatest form of flattery but in business I call that stealing. And there are many out there trying to steal your hard work so that they may profit. The impact of having something stolen could be either a minor annoyance or could literally put you out of business.

There are four things that could be stolen from you that could have dire consequences to your business:

1) Physical Assets
2) Key Personnel
3) Key Customers
4) Intellectual Property

And we are going to outline a few ways to protect yourself, and your company, from these scoundrels.

Just the other night Rita woke me up at 2:09am and whispered in my ear "Will, don't move but I think I hear someone downstairs". Now let me say that my wife and I have been trained in handling weapons. And one of our training courses was an in-home invasion session on how to handle intruders using the advantageous angles throughout the house. But, this was not a dress rehearsal...at least it didn't appear to be.

Let me release a little anxiety by saying that it was a false alarm. But the way my heart was racing signified that I was ready for the real thing. In your business, Pirate Scoundrels attack in the same manner; they can be very stealthy and move when your guard is down. They normally go after only the valuables just like a burglar. And they know all the techniques to evade the most sophisticated burglar system. In order to reduce the ramifications of such an event, you need protection.

Protection can be had in many different manners like homeowners insurance. For a home invasion, Rita and I took weapons training as a form of insurance; along with a dog and a burglar system for protection. But the most important form of insurance is your anticipation of negative events. Keep in mind that a loss is part of operating any business so it's your job to expect it and prepare for it. And it's incumbent upon you not to let it harden your heart or affect your attitude toward employees, customers and the general public.

Keep in mind that the easiest things for others to steal from you are your physical assets. And in business, you will need to make some financial investment in equipment, facility, supplies and inventory. So a very important step is to have a very capable insurance agent who understands business. In a later chapter we will address the importance of having the right people in the right places and a good insurance agent is one of them.

Do not skimp on this my friends because it is crucial to protecting your assets. And you truly don't appreciate the significance that a building, vehicle or any other asset has to your business until it is no longer there. Let me share a time where the proper insurance agent was paramount to our business succeeding.

In the fall of 2010, our school bus was vandalized. The bus was used to transport 48 students to the local school system each and everyday; morning & afternoons. Then in the dead of night, someone had stolen our catalytic converters (a device made with platinum) which rendered the bus inoperable. Because we had an agent who spent 20 years in the industry, we talked about what level of insurance we should have for all potential outcomes. Suffice it to say, we had a replacement bus within hours while the other was being repaired.   And our parents didn't even feel the pain of our loss. This may not sound like a big deal to you but try to find a 50 passenger school bus with a few hours notice.

Now, let's address our thoughts on protecting your key employees and customers. When you hire an employee, you make a major financial investment in that person to bring them up to a certain level of productivity. You invest in their training, benefits, tools, etc. And for those you promote to leadership positions, well you've invested even more training and time to get them to the point where they can run a portion of your business in an effective manner.   Now all of a sudden, your friendly neighborhood competitor decides to steal him away by offering something different. I've been on both sides of that equation as an employee and as a business owner. One makes you feel elated and the other deflates you.

In some entrepreneur's eyes, this is another form of stealing. When this subject was brought up in one of our monthly meetings, a member likened this to having the kid down the street steal your girlfriend. His point was that it's no big deal and it's just a part of growing up. Okay, I could see the comparison he was trying to make but this is your business so it's different. But let's say that this employee starts off as a "girlfriend" in this comparison but later becomes a "wife". And she has crucial company knowledge that could make you vulnerable to the kid (competitor) down the street.

In the analogy, a girlfriend is like an entry-level employee and a wife is like a key manager who knows everything about how you run your business. She knows how you make money, your proprietary business systems, trade secrets and the combination to the safe. Not to mention that she has a personal relationship with all your important customers. The key person is in a position to serve the business well or destroy it with some carefully placed land mines about your operations. You need to protect yourself and your company.

Here is where a good lawyer comes into play to keep you protected from this scoundrel. The government has many programs in place to protect our employees from harm to their person and their livelihood. They have worker's compensation insurance should they get hurt on the job and unemployment insurance should we have to lay off someone due to shortage of work. And employers have health insurance for them and their families and COBRA to extend that coverage should they leave. But it's your responsibility to exercise the same zest and zeal to insure your company's success by strategically placing barriers in areas where the employees could harm the business.

Each employee in our companies has signed a non-compete clause in our employment agreement. That means they are not allowed to pursue employment that could jeopardize the viability of our business. If they decide to leave us they are not allowed to take with them any tool, customer or knowledge that could hurt the business. We do not begrudge those who seek to leave us for new employment. As a matter of fact, we use it as an opportunity to learn so that we can be a better place to work. It's just that only you are empowered to protect your remaining employees and customers from harm. Remember that we are talking about protection here.

Patrons & Passerbys Scoundrel Protection

We should never forget that we are in business to serve. That means serving our customers and employees to give each party the best experience possible. A happy employee will go beyond the call of duty to take care of the customer. And a happy customer will continue to do business with us and even referring other customers. But at times, these two parties want to unjustly serve themselves to the detriment of the business owner. We need to insure against that.

Again, a good lawyer will save you a tremendous amount of money and headache over the course of your business operation. Until recently, I would literally hit the ceiling each and every time I got a legal bill. I would say to Rita, "This law firm is killing me.

Where's the value?" And this went on for years until a few incidents happened that demonstrated their true value.

First, Passerbys Scoundrels are employees looking to get more than they work for. Now would be a good time to make the distinction between a Passerby and a good employee. For the good employee you put in systems to protect them from harm and for the other you put in systems to protect your company from them. We've put in many processes during the interview process to determine who is, or is not, a good fit but still the Passerby can get past us. But when they do get in, it doesn't take long before they show their true colors.

Even though you may do everything to give your employees the best (i.e. working environment, health & dental, childcare, vacation/sick days, etc.), there will be some who still want more and will pursue legal action to get it. Remember, our legal system doesn't discern between a legitimate lawsuit and a frivolous one; all are invited to the courtroom with you paying for the party through your attorney's legal bills.

Second, Patron Scoundrels are customers that will never be happy no matter how hard you work to serve them. As business owners we have an obligation to our customers; we should always cover an accident that happens in the course of business. This is a part of your fiduciary agreement with the customer. The scoundrel that we are referring to is the patron who doesn't want any sort of equitable remedy but a large piece of your hind quarters.

The proper business lawyer along with a good insurance agent, are excellent in developing a shield for your business. This shield will protect you against the slings and arrows of day-to-day business operations. It comes in the form of documents which will govern your agreements with all who enter your business. Please keep in mind that this shield will not stop people from attempting to sue you, but it will lower their probability of success. And when these documents are done properly, an opposing attorney will review them and decide that it is not worth their time to pursue you legally. When that happens, your lawyer has just validated his existence.

Crucial documents like an "Employment Agreement" will protect you from a disgruntled employee. A "Customer Agreement or Handbook" will protect you from an over zealous customer who may be seeking more satisfaction than they deserve. These are just some of the important documents that you must have to protect yourself. In order to develop a bulletproof vest around your business you must make sure your communication with your lawyer is honest and direct. Do everything prescribed by her when running your business in conjunction with these documents. So when you are pursued legally (and you will be), you have an excellent chance of prevailing.

Posterity Scoundrel Protection

When we sat down to talk about this chapter we felt a little……should I say mean when grouping our kids in with scoundrels. Yet there is nothing like money to bring out the worst in the people you love; namely your children.

"I will do anything for my babies" was the vernacular used by my mother when we were growing up. And she instilled in me, and my sisters, that it was our duty to do the best for our children. With our work ethic and the success of our business dealings, we are able to give our sons a standard of living far beyond anything we had as children. But are we really doing them any favors by giving them everything that we can?

It became clear to me that even the best intentioned parents could unknowingly be raising a scoundrel. I recall a cookout at a neighbor's house last summer where we sat around the pool, drinking great wine and eating even better food with some friends in our neighborhood.

As I dangled my legs by the edge of the pool next to my wife, we overheard the homeowners' 14 year old say to our oldest son, "I have a college fund too but my dad is going to leave me all his money and company when he dies; I will be set. What about your dad?" My son Anthony, treading water in the deep end of the pool looked over to us at first then took a pause and replied, "My dad said he will pay for my college but leave me very little money when he dies. That's ok, because I will make my own."

We smiled at each other and gave our son an affirming nod. Though the neighbor kid gave us a puzzled look, our son was very clear on what was going to happen. But more importantly, he was more than okay with it because he had been told many times of our position on leaving money to him and his brother.

We have witnessed first hand how parents can create a scoundrel kid. They give their children everything they want either because they have the means or maybe because they feel guilty about something. In either situation, they trade money for time not spent with the kids. Because of this, these kids tend to feel entitled and have no idea what hard work is. And they don't understand the value of money.

This chapter isn't just on how to protect your wealth from scoundrel kids but about how to protect your kids from being scoundrels in the first place. When you get to the chapter entitled "Legacy: Your Children's Financial Education", you will find more details on what you can do to raise a child that is not a scoundrel. Here are some of our rules for raising kids so that they don't become scoundrels:

1.) *Must do your chores around the house without pay.*
   This is the beginning of understanding teamwork and there isn't a single business person worth his/her salt who doesn't understand how crucial teamwork is to success. My sons are apart of Team Scott and everyone has a role. The team is counting on each member to do their job. And if the job is not done, then the team suffers. The privilege of a roof over your head, clothing, warmth and food are repaid by doing your chores.

2.) Must do designated work in order to earn income.
Cleaning the garage, babysitting, washing cars are some of the duties that we have designated as paying jobs. So if you need a new skateboard or cell phone, seek out these jobs and complete them.

3.) Never say you cannot afford something. If you want it, use your creativity to find a way to pay for it.
We don't believe in the idea of scarcity. These thoughts are limiting and take away your power to create your own reality. We want our sons to have all they desire, but we want them to work for it. The entrepreneur spirit has its beginnings within desire and from that place we feel our sons can have anything they want. Here is where our oldest learned the value of leverage.

4.) Don't look to others to satisfy your wants. Work with others and they will help you achieve your goals.
Empowerment is the agent that will strengthen the backbone of your children. We must teach our kids that the method of extending their hands to mom & dad for money to get what they want is a tool of incompetence. We feel its okay when they are little ones but it's during those years that we open their eyes to their strengths so that their teenage years are more independent. Put them in situations where they can learn to lead people and achieve their goals through the team. Organized team sports and Boy Scouts are the venues that we have our boys participate and there is where they learn to serve others and reach a goal worthy of their efforts.

Let's assume that the lessons that we want our children to learn are not mastered before they reach legal age. Sorry to say this but there is a high probability that they will leave your house not fully understanding some an important lesson until a new teacher appears. And that new teacher's name is LIFE. And if our children decide to take the same maturation course we took, then we've developed a protection strategy for those scoundrels.

We sat down with an estate lawyer and asked about the best way to handle our children and our wealth. We discussed our concerns and our fears. Because of his wealth of knowledge in this area and the years of experience, we received excellent advice on how to protect our asset from scoundrel kids.

One method was to develop a trust that would allow our kids to rely on themselves and grow their own financial knowledge before they received a single dollar. Our plan would allow our kids to receive a portion of the trust in three intervals based on age. We are assuming that as they mature the probability of them needing the trust will diminish. This staggered plan will give them the money at a point after they've leveraged the financial education we gave them. Then, if needed, they could invest that money to grow more money.

But here is the true protection strategy. We are not protecting our money from our children; we are giving them a firm financial education so they will not desire our money. This is the biggest gift that we can give our children as parents. Letting our kids in on meetings with our banker, lawyer, accountant and coaches is the precursor to learning about how money and business works.

Teaching them how to read a profit & loss statement and cash flow statement are vital in doing your due diligence in any business and they are learning that first hand. The art of managing and leading people who work for you and the art of selling your ideas to important partners cannot be learned in textbooks. So the best protection from the Posterity Scoundrel is to teach them how money works and give them opportunity to strengthen their newly found financial muscle. We will talk more about this in the chapter titled "Legacy: Your Family's Financial Education"

Mom & Pop's Key Points:

1. Insurance is the most valuable instrument in protecting your investment, so get good advice from wise professionals.
2. Knowledge is your best form of protection.
3. Teach your children early and they will not become scoundrels.

Mom & Pop's To Do's:

4. Begin to interview lawyers, accountants, insurance agents. Look for those who are entrepreneurs and work with entrepreneurs.
5. Never put your business or it's assets in your personal name. Select the right entity with your lawyer and accountant.
6. Join local groups with like-minded people so you can network and develop leads for your business. Consider *Am Spirit*.
7. Take your kids on all meetings where it makes sense.

SEEKING COACHES & BOARD OF DIRECTORS

My mother would always tell me that she can tell a lot about a person by talking to the guys they hang around. She wanted to make sure that the kids I hung out with stayed out of trouble and did well in school. "Birds of a feather flock together" is the old adage that came to mind each and every time we had this conversation.

As usual, Mom was right and I took careful guard of who I hung out with because trouble was so easy to find when I was with the wrong type. The same philosophy can be applicable building your business. In this situation, your main concern is not being around people who could get you into trouble, but being around people that could get you into success.

As you start your business, you are going down a road that is new to you. Most likely, no one in your family or even closest friend has had any quantifiable success as an entrepreneur. Maybe you've heard of someone who started a business and you decided you could do it too. Just remember that it doesn't matter how you start; what matters is how you finish. And to finish well in meeting your goals on the way to your exit strategy (which we will address in a later chapter), you must bring in a good coach.

A good coach serves the purpose of assisting you in areas of your life where deficiencies are stalling your success. What we discovered over the years is that no part of your life stands in perfect isolation of another part. The whole of who you are cannot be compartmentalized and nor should it be in order to succeed in life. Each aspect of your life has to be enriched in order for the other parts to have the same opportunity for enrichment. If you allow apart of your life to stall and atrophy, then it shuts off any potential power to be used in another.

An example can be found in my life. I allowed the discontentment in my corporate career to spill over into other parts of my life. Dissatisfaction with work eventually led to lack of exercise which affected my health; the weight gain then affected our love life and family life. And then that despair leads me on a path that didn't include a relationship with God, so my spiritual life suffered. It became somewhat of a death spiral for me and Rita didn't know how to help. Then one day I made the decision to hire a life coach to help me out.

I hired a life coach and it has made all the difference for me, my wife, our kids, my faith and our business. I tell you this very personal story with my wife's permission because I want to make it emphatically clear that you should not start this journey alone; you need a guide. Someone who has experience in taking the path that is so new to you. Let's say that you've made the decision to earn a spot on the US Olympic team and you had just two short years to make the team. What would you do? The wise decision would be to recruit a coach with experience in helping people make the Olympic team. We must do the same for our lives and our business.

We have found that you must find a coach, or coaches, to lead you in these critical areas of your life:

1. Spiritual/Mental Life
2. Physical Life
3. Love Life
4. Family/Community Life
5. Business/Career Life
6. Financial Life

These are all the areas of your life that makes you the whole of who you are. Not a single area can be neglected without it having tremendous impact on the other areas.

Some may say that all these areas do not have to be operating at 100% efficiency in order for you to be complete and actualized; we totally concur. But the true message is that not a single one can be 100% shut down without the ripple effect being felt in all other remaining parts.

This rule has been proven in the lives of so many and it cannot be broken without tremendous ramifications. We know of a couple who had a successful business and other assets that made money without them working. Both were athletic (marathoner and yoga enthusiast) and members of the church. But in all their efforts, they neglected each other and their love life suffered. He had an affair (death of love life & family life) with someone in the church (death of spiritual community life). Then eventually divorced and sold the business to go their separate ways (death of business life & financial life).

This is the most tragic situation that we've seen in our journey of entrepreneurship. But our point here is that all areas are crucial and you are simply rolling the dice each day you neglect a part of your life. It may have a short fuse and blow up right in your face or it could be a ticking time bomb that has a calendar for a clock. Anyway you slice it; you are the only one putting off the inevitable.

For the purposes of the book we will only concentrate on Business/Career and Financial Life. We realized very early in our process that we didn't know enough to get to the level we wanted, so we decided to seek a coach. Since we didn't know anyone with the expertise we needed, we looked for coaches on the web and in books.

There are many people out there who have written books in the areas of business and finance. Many have started from humble beginnings and some have been surrounded by success since birth. It doesn't matter their background as much as their knowledge. When you start off on this very important step finding good advice is paramount.

So go to the bookstore and look for books on entrepreneurship, business, motivation, finance, etc. Look for people on the best seller's list and check out the reference sections of each of their books. You will find a few authors that you like and then try to read all of their material. They will likely become a de facto standard for you in the area of business that most concerns you.

We've made a few authors our coaches via all their written and audio material and they have given us a good start on our journey to entrepreneurship. Some of our favorite author coaches are Michael Gerber, Robert Kiyosaki, Napoleon Hill, Anthony Robbins, Donald Trump, John C. Maxwell and Stephen Covey.

After you've selected and studied your author coaches, it's time to seek human coaches that you can meet with and strategize with on growing your business. By this time, you are aware of the value of coaching and what type of coach you need to get to the next level. Keep in mind that you are not necessarily looking for someone who thinks like you. As one of our coaches used to say to us, "In business, if you have two people in the room and they both agree then one is unnecessary."

You are looking for someone who challenges your thoughts and beliefs. You are looking for someone that pushes you past your comfort level to get things done. This coach is most likely not a friend and this coach is not always a gentle soul. This person is driven by your goals and your timeframe and is willing to push all necessary buttons to get you there. Don't look for this person to do it for you or to offer you important contacts from their personal circle of influencers. This is not their job, nor their true value to you.

You must do this building process yourself and you must cultivate the contacts yourself because this is ultimately your success. This can be a major stumbling block for so many couples and they tend to stop right here. Great businesses with great ideas "clothes line" themselves early in the journey when they don't seek good coaching. In most situations, a good coach will open their contacts to you in areas that will serve your learning and advancement, but only at the right time.

When we decided to seek a coach we made a commitment to ourselves that we would only seek people who have started a business or have coached successful business owners. Through these two criteria we would get real world experience. Someone with the scars from the battles of business or tremendous experience in helping other entrepreneurs heal their wounds of business. You cannot find this in a book or a college level course.

We knew this was the right starting point for us, but we just didn't know where to turn first. So we started with SCORE.org which is a part of Small Business Administration. Here you will find a group of retired executives from all types of businesses. What a wealth of business knowledge from people who actually did what we were looking to do. And the service was free of charge.

Then we went to our accountant and lawyer. We had interviewed these people before we made them apart of our team. And during that process we ask them for references so that we could understand how they did business. This served two purposes: 1) it helped us understand their level of expertise, creativity and professionalism and 2) it helped us find new potential coaches and mastermind members.

This group of business owners spans the spectrum of every type of business imaginable. We talked and met with people who were married, single, just starting their business and some who had made their exit. And within this group we developed coaches that helped us grow our business.

Keep in mind that the coaches we developed didn't take us under their wings because they were just awesome people. Don't walk into this process thinking that altruism is the motivating force within the minds of these people; though for some it is. They're business people and they have taught themselves a lesson that is extremely important in business…. their time has value. They are always seeking value.

So when we search for a coach/mentor we first seek to understand their business and what is important to them. And then we ask ourselves if we can offer some value to them in those crucial areas. It could be our contacts, some information we have from our efforts in the field or our willingness to just be another set of eyes and ears in a specific endeavor. No matter what, we must show value to that person in order to ask for something of value. And we have found that most business people have a great sense of fair play and they always want to give value when they have received it. When this happens, we are confident that we've earned the right to ask for guidance and we have yet to be turned down.

Then there are those people where chemistry is high and you just hit-it-off from the first time you meet. You want to extend yourselves to each other with no anticipation of reciprocation. These are, in our opinion, rare and magical encounters because we've only witnessed a few. When you find a coach like this you must count yourself among the lucky ones and work diligently to show value. We found one of our first coaches/mentors in a similar manner. Let me tell you how it came to be.

I just took a promotion from Hewlett-Packard to move back to Cleveland after a two year stint in Toledo and my girlfriend (Rita) encouraged me to buy a small townhouse in a nearby suburb. My next door neighbor was a recently divorced gentleman who owned a manufacturing business. He came by to introduce himself and marvel at my car (Merkur Scorpio) and my tires (Pirelli). I knew more about cars than tires so he asked if I wanted to see his vintage Corvette. And a friendship began were we played racquetball, rode motorcycles and fished as often as we could.

We stayed in touch over the years and he really demonstrated his friendship when I told him about our desire to start a business. I still remember the moment when I told him this because he gave me a look of both excitement and caution. He said "Don't make any major financial moves until we talk. If I can't help you in the process then I can find someone who will." It was at that time he began to give me advice and direction.

To continue the conversation on coaches; please do not be afraid to pay for coaching. This was a hard lesson for me at first because I was confident that those people were just there to take my money.

This was residue of my Perverted Wealth Logic and this thought had to go. I remind you that something of value will cost something of value. You are an entrepreneur and your business will be selling something and the value you will require is a fair price. This is the life blood of business.

There are many great companies that offer coaching that will serve you in growing your business. We have hired such coaches in the past and we have had quantifiable results. That makes us extreme proponents of these professionals. Caution: do your homework and talk to past clients to understand what they received and if their expectations were met.

Board of Directors

If you're like me, you are probably saying to yourself right now, *"I don't need a board of directors, I'm not listed on the NASDAQ or New York Stock Exchange"*. Those were the exact words I told our coach when he suggested this very important group of people as advisors. Besides, BODs (Board of Directors) have been known to fire their company presidents in the past. If I'm not mistaken, wasn't it the BODs of Apple Computer that fired Steve Jobs as their president; the company he founded. *"Well, that will not happen to me. I will not let some group of people I selected tell me that I must leave my own company!"*

Can you tell that I got a little ahead of myself with that train of thought? These things normally happen with big companies that are publicly traded. The point here is that you should consider a BODs to help guide you on critical decisions.

As your business grows you will find yourself faced with critical "go/no go" business decisions that should never be made by you two alone. You were the ones with the intestinal fortitude to start this but you need more than your brain power if you want to grow it. These critical decisions have to be made with a process that takes in all options and ramifications. Trust me when I say this…you and your wife are not qualified to do this alone.

Your BODs should be made of people with expertise in all critical areas of your business. This level of expertise must be in industry, legal, finance, management, operations, insurance, etc. They can listen to your plans for the next 90 days to the next 5 years and offer sound advice to protect you and insure success. We have "confidentiality agreements" with each member of our board and we make it explicitly clear that they are not to sit on the board of any of our competitors.

We don't make any mission critical decision unless it is brought to our quarterly board meeting. If we are looking to acquire another business, buy a building, implement a 401k, install a new back office systems, hire a new manager or even select a new landscape service; it all goes before the board. They have been instrumental in helping us do our due diligence before any decision has been made in these areas.

There was a time that we didn't have a BODs and we made decisions that didn't serve us as well as we had hoped. I recall a time when we decided to buy a property for expansion. We bought a lot with an old home on it and we wanted to tear it down for new construction. I thought I was smart because I managed to secure it at a residential price six months prior to a zoning change to commercial. So I bought a commercial property at residential pricing… I'd say that I did well on this transaction. But here's where the mistakes were made in which my BODs could have helped me.

I decided to save the money on demolition and have the fire department use it for a training exercise and burn it to the ground. In the process of completing all the necessary paperwork, the fire department contacted the EPA (Environmental Protection Agency) to have it tested for asbestos; normal protocol in these situations but I didn't know that. The EPA discovered asbestos and this cost me an additional $20k for asbestos abatement on top of the debris removal after the fire training. You will not believe how HOT I was to discover that I had to pay this (no pun intended).

If I had consulted my current real estate advisor, I would have known about a rule that allows residential homes with asbestos in shingles to be demolished without any abatement cost. She would have advised me not to contact the fire department because it would have been incumbent upon them to contact the EPA. With her guidance, I would have contracted for a demolition only with a cost of $5,000. This turned out to be a $15,000 lesson.

In regards to the same deal, we didn't consult our BODs on tax abatement and it cost us far more money in real estate taxes than we should have paid. You may recall when we mentioned that taxes are your single largest expense and you must have sound advice in order to lower them. We were just so excited about expansion that it never entered our minds as we crafted the deal. Because of the zoning change, the real estate taxes increased two fold. A considerable jump I would say.

I thought I was being like Donald Trump in negotiating such a hard deal on the property that I didn't look at all costs of the deal. To get to the heart of the lesson, we later got our accountant, lawyer and real estate advisor (BOD) in on the transaction soon after closing and they helped us apply for tax abatement because we were bringing new jobs to the area. Just this one simple move saved us thousands of dollars per year.

Also keep in mind that if you've chosen the right people for your BODs, you have not only selected individuals with expertise, but you also have people of influence. Our BODs are vital members of the business community where we operate and they know many business people and government officials. And just by the virtue of sitting on our board, they made their network of contacts ours too.

It was through our accountant that we started our first mastermind group. A mastermind group is a select group of like minded individuals with a commitment to each other to assist in reaching goals and holding each other accountable. Any resource within the group may become a resource for anyone in the group in order to reach their goal. We setup this group with a mission in mind: "To assist each other in becoming multi-millionaires with multiple streams of income in order that we may serve our God, family & community and leave a legacy of abundant empowerment."

With our mastermind group we felt like we extended our BODs because we found more capable advisors who held us accountable to reaching our goals. And the brain power that swirled around the room during our sessions was so excited and contagious. Ideas and creativity were so intense that some new business ventures and revenue generation opportunities often came from us getting together. Keeping company with like minded people will be the difference in the success of your business.

Mom & Pop's Key Points:

1. Seek coaches at the bookstore and library first.
2. Remember to offer value to anyone you would like as a coach.
3. Chose the best in their discipline to be on your BOD.

Mom & Pop's To Do's:

4. Start with a trusted accountant when beginning your search for coaches & BOD.
5. SCORE.org is invaluable.
6. Don't be afraid to use social media to find like-minded people. Your next coach maybe a click away.

GROWING YOUR TEAM

We talked a little about leverage earlier in the book and how, when used properly, it can yield significant results. While some may say that the mastery of leveraging money (also known as debt) is the most important skill, we say that the mastery of leveraging people's time and effort is just as important. You cannot be in more than one place at one time and you cannot do everything at once. This is where having the right people in the right places doing the right things is the difference between success and failure.

You may start your venture with your spouse but within a very short period, you will have to bring people on to get more things done. You will have to hire those to do certain tasks so you may do those things that offer the most value. Those lesser valued activities could be cleaning the floors or cutting the grass or shoveling the snow from the sidewalks. You two are the strategic heads of this enterprise and though you may have done these things at first, your business demands more of you now.

In our consulting business, we thought it would be easy to find good people that could write software code. Trust me when I say it takes a certain type of personality to sit down at a computer and write software for many hours a day. These individuals don't seek, nor desire, much contact with the customer or others because that is not their skill set. They simply enjoyed going to their computers and typing away. That was all our business model demanded of them and it all worked out perfectly.

The problem presented itself when we decided to expand to take on more clients. We had to promote a person to project manager immediately. And this position would be the interface with the client, which in the past was exclusively Rita's role. Then she could be freed up to go off to do another project. Suffice it to say, it didn't work and the clients threatened to fire us unless we brought Rita back. And our new project manager felt impotent in this new role and wanted to leave.

We had to revert back to our old way of doing business which unfortunately almost killed Rita's spirit. There has to be a better way? And as we said in *Clarity of What*; we set out to find it by talking to our coaches and reading books in this area. The people we knew, who had similar obstacles at some point in time, told us horror stories which contained invaluable lessons. Coupled with our own real world experience, we managed to put together three key points of emphasis within the hiring process:

Mom & Pop's Points of Emphasis
In the Hiring Process

1. Attracting: *Hire attitude first, then aptitude.*
2. Training: *Develop an air tight/water tight business system and train them to run it.*
3. Retaining: *Understand each employee's gain.*

Hiring Attitude First, Then Aptitude

I remember in high school our freshman football coach saying, *"Bring a football player to the field and I can coach him any football skill but I can't coach desire, he must bring that with him."* That was my first lesson on how important attitude is to your success. Attitude is your steering wheel that will guide you to your destination or send you on a bumpy road to nowhere.

As sales manager and director of sales in the software industry, I knew the value of attitude when selecting a member of our sales team. When in the trenches of a deal there are times when things look their darkest and despite of all the effort, you may end with a loss. Staying in that moment doesn't serve you so you must enter every deal as though the outcome has already been realized…you've won the deal. That is attitude.

At one time in our schools, Rita had seen a trend of deficiency in our staff in areas that she never thought she would. She had trained our managers to select people with extreme diligence. Yet, we were seeing a significant portion of our new hires not measuring up to our standards. They just didn't go beyond the call of duty to give our customer a great customer experience. In our schools, we don't work for customer satisfaction, we drive for customer delight. And our staff is on the front line of that mission. But we just were not seeing it done in the same fashion our customers had grown accustom to receiving.

We notice that some of the staff didn't appear to be happy at our schools. When we conducted one-on-one's with these people to ascertain what we could do to make them happy, each one stated that they were happy. I can remember one instance where Rita said to a teacher, "You maybe happy it's just that you forgot to tell your face."

These events brought back a memory of going to Disney World with our kids on spring break. We had a great time and marveled at the level of customer service we received from the cast members (staff). They were committed to giving us an extraordinary customer experience. We wanted Young Explorers Schools to be just like that, so we decided to enroll in an Executive Seminar Series held by Disney on customer satisfaction. Let me first say that Disney has figured it out and has an excellent plan of execution. We recommend their training series whole-heartedly.

There was a particular session in this two-day event where the class had a chance to address our personal concerns in the area of hiring. All attendees were of one unanimous view that Disney had great employees and the good feelings the customers felt in each park, hotel or restaurant left a lasting impression. Then one of the attendees asked the trainer this. *"How does Disney train their people to care so much and be so happy?"* At that moment, Rita whispered in my ear that this was the most important question in her mind and this lady had just stolen it. Nevertheless, we got the answer that we were seeking though it wasn't quite what we were expecting.

When posed with the question on how Disney trains their people to care so much and be so happy, the answer came back with a melodic, "**we don't**." Now that was a surprise and a hush fell over the crowd. They weren't expecting that either. But in that moment of pause it started to make sense. How can you train a personality trait? Just like you can't coach desire; you either have it or you don't.

The trainer then said "The reason our people are so caring and happy is because we only hire caring and happy people." It was as simple as that. No Disney pixy dust or Mickey Mouse magic; they simply hire people that fit that profile. As the training session went on, we received primers on how their hiring process worked to leverage the desired results. We also learned some techniques on how to select the right people. When the class was over, we packed our bags and took our new knowledge home to test it out.

When we sat down with our management staff and developed a new step in the selection process for new teachers. With the help of this training, we developed new tools to help our managers ascertain each candidate's level of caring and happiness. Before the Disney training, we didn't have the foggiest idea on how to do this. So we took some of their core principles and blended it in with our business systems. Below is a description of a method we incorporated into our in-take process.

Once a candidate completed our employment application and took part in an instrument (test) to understand their level of expertise; we would then select a short list of candidates to interview. The process is fairly rudimentary and most of us have been through it more than once in our careers. The difference in our process is that we can now separate the happy and caring people from the unhappy and uncaring people within minutes of walking through the door for their first interview.

Here was our first step in the process. The moment they walked into the building we immediately look them in the eye and gave them our standard greeting. We looked immediately for eye contact and a smile; nothing else. Innately happy people will always greet people with an approachable smile in most situations. This can rarely be faked, but some people are expert interviewers and may give us what we want while in the presence of management. So then we setup the next step in the process.

The second step occurs when we ask each candidate to sit in the lobby to wait for their interview. Within minutes of them taking in their surroundings, we begin our second step in their evaluation. We have a teacher walk through the lobby toward the office. She stops and introduces herself in our standard greeting. If the candidate gets up from her seat and greets the teacher with a warm and happy smile she will be allowed to continue on the interview process. After that interaction, the teacher would then continue to the office and report on the candidate's response.

The last and final step in order to have a face-to-face interview with the Director is crucial in helping us uncover those candidates who will go beyond the call-of-duty. Please understand that this process doesn't guarantee any candidate's level of success, it simply gives us a good insight into a candidate's inclinations in real world situations.

Here we will have another teacher walk through the lobby on her way to a nearby classroom. We make sure that she is carrying something that has multiple pieces (i.e. puzzle, building blocks, balls etc.). Then she *accidentally* drops them to the ground and gives a low sound of distress. Then she will bend down to take her time in retrieving the items. Here we are looking for the candidate who is willing to serve and go beyond herself to serve even though it may have no immediate benefit to her or him. If the candidate immediately gets up to assist the teacher, then there is a high probability that we have a good candidate.

This may all sound a little stealthy but having the right people on your team is one of the most important activities you will do for your business. These people will represent you and your business when you are not around so we must choose very carefully.

Develop an Air Tight/Water Tight Business System and Train Them How to Run It.

You can no more ask an employee to be someone she's not anymore than you can ask her to do a job they haven't been trained to do. Too many times we've sat with our heads in our hands when an employee has done something wrong. When on the surface, it appeared to be so obvious if exercising common sense. "What were they thinking" is what Rita would say and I would say "they weren't thinking". We knew that we could not expand the business if our staff is left to their own devices to perform at a level we require.

We've developed our business around a system that would make us similar to a franchise business. A system for assuring that we would get the same desired result in every aspect of our business: accounting, purchasing supplies & equipment, etc. But the most important systems we developed was around how to train our staff to deliver the same quality experience no matter who the customer, the employee or the location.

We created a training system with three things in mind:

Young Explorers Montessori's Optimum Aim

1. *Everything we do must delight the customer's sense of sight, sound, smell, touch and taste.*
2. *Everything we do must be in an effort to distinguish our brand from our competition.*
3. *Everything we do must be easily repeatable and understood by the employee.*
4. *Everything we do must be done to perfection in order to reward our customers, suppliers and ourselves.*

We knew that we had to separate ourselves from our competitors by giving our customers an experience that was far better than anything they could receive anywhere else. In our schools, we knew the training of the teachers was important and we knew the curriculum was also paramount. But it's the small things that our competitors don't pay attention to that add value to our schools. And that is where we developed the mantra "Delight Customer's Senses."

This mantra keeps us all on guard to anything that dulls our customer's senses when interacting with Young Explorers. And it empowers each staff member to correct it if standards weren't being met. If any staff member saw garbage in the parking lot it was removed by that staff member immediately; garbage in the parking lot is unpleasant to the sense of sight. If the building didn't smell up to our standard, a teacher would be empowered to change the automatic air freshener, empty diaper pale, open a window or inform the cleaning crew; bad scents offend the sense of smell.

So we developed our business training system where each and every activity can be aligned with delighting the senses. If your job is to turn on the classical music each morning before the school opens, you are aware of the value it has in delighting our customer's sense of sound. And when you understand the value and your importance in its delivery; you are more likely to carry it out with a sense of ownership.

Secondly, we've made sure that we put systems in our business that are easily repeatable and understood by the employee. Our coaches instructed us on how to develop a great roadmap for this business system. And one of the major points we received from this training was a business owner must do everything possible to remove discretion from the employees in the business.

We're not saying that we don't want our people to think. It's just that we only want them to think of one thing; their job. And their job is to deliver on our mission. When a situation arises; the teacher will do the activity that they were trained to do in that scenario; nothing more and nothing less. We've train our management to make the day-to-day decisions and trained our staff to do the day-to-day job. Removing this discretion from them has lightened their spirits as they tackle the job of educating children and delighting parents.

As an example, when a parent becomes upset for any reason; teachers are not trained to handle that. Our managers are the only individuals trained to de-escalate and find resolution in the quickest fashion possible. So when this scenario presents itself, the teacher makes an empathetic statement that they have been trained to deliver and then walks the parent to the Director's office. Then the teacher and Director will work together to find resolution and regain customer delight.

Understand Each Employee's Gain

We had a gentleman in our mastermind group once who said that just being employed with his company should be exciting enough to keep a person motivated. "We are the best in the business" is what he said as though that should be enough. I thought that he was kidding but he appeared very serious. His words confirmed why he kept losing key people after just a few years in business.

As we look back we realize that we may have been working with that same arrogance because we were losing key people after just a few years too. We also noticed that some who were once excellent employees slowly began to deteriorate to the point that we had to ask them to leave. What would cause a once great employee to turn into someone who just appeared to stop caring? We had to take responsibility for this drastic change.

Bob reminded us that human nature is prevalent in all areas of business and that it is in everyone's nature to desire more. We call this **Your Desired Gain** and everyone's gain is different and it's their motivating factor. We exited the corporate cyclone to become entrepreneurs because there was something that we wanted to gain: freedom, control and wealth. As we look at the people on our team, we asked each what they wanted out of this job, this company and their lives. It may sound a little touchy feely but it's important to let them know we care; because we do.

What we desire to gain out of this business can only be attained through the leverage of our people. So why not use our leverage to help them gain something more than just a paycheck. As married business partners, we sit down to do this same exercise once a year to see if anything has changed. I'm consistently surprise when Rita has changed her gains through the years. But things change as you get older so what you desire changes as well. That is why you must stay on top of each employee's desired gains on a consistent basis.

We had an employee who had been with us since our first day of business. She was instrumental in getting the business started and growing it significantly in just four short years. And during that time we constantly inquired about her desired gains from this business. She liked beginning her work day after 9am so she could get her kids on the school bus and she wanted to enroll her infant at no cost. There were other desired gains and most of them we could easily meet with no degradation to the business.

Her performance always improved and she kept adding value to the business so we had no problem adding value to her. Then around the fourth year with us, we noted a marked decrease in job performance and wanted to know why. She had been splitting her time between our school and her effort to start her own. She wanted us to know that her heart was no longer in this school. We understood and sent her off with our blessing and any coaching she needed to get this new venture off the ground. No, we are not advocating that you should help your employee leave to become your competitor but it is always better to show character and integrity.

As her business grew, she referred customers to us that didn't fit her target market and we did the same. This new relationship caused our customer base to grow and increased our bottom line. Here is a great example of how understanding someone's desired gain has helped our business grow.

Let's not ignore the obvious gain of every employee; money. People work to fulfill many needs and dreams in life and money is the means to that end. We don't begrudge the desire for money when you add value; as a matter of fact we consider it mandatory. This is why we have MBOs (Management by Objectives) in our process. These MBOs clearly state what hurdles have to be cleared in order to receive a bonus; which is usually every quarter. These hurdles are things that add more value to the business, employees and customers.

This gives our people a sense of ownership in the company as well as a sense that they can impact their yearly income. Many ideas and innovations have come from our incentive plans and it has been well worth the effort.

Mom & Pop's Key Points:

1. Entrepreneurs get things done through people.
2. Hire attitude, develop business system and understand each employees gain.
3. Aim for Customer Delight and referrals will come.

Mom & Pop's To Do's:

4. Read "The 21 Irrefutable Laws of Leadership" by John C. Maxwell to understand what it takes to lead a team to success.
5. Read the book "Hug Your People" by Jack Mitchell.
6. Consider using JOBehaviors and Kolbe to select the best possible candidates for your business.
7. Design a "Gain Plan" for each of your staff and track it on an annual basis.

MULTIPLE STREAMS OF INCOME

So you've got your business clicking on all eight cylinders and you have it throwing off money every month. Congratulations but don't think that you've arrived yet. This is only one source of cash flow and in order to deal with the ups and downs of business and economic cycles, you need multiple streams of income. Most of us sleep better at night when both parents are gainfully employed; if one is laid off then the other one can pay the bills. Even as an entrepreneur, you will eventually feel the same way about having just one source of cash flow.

Before we start this chapter, let me state what I hope is obvious. Just because you've had success starting your current business doesn't automatically give you the "Midas Touch" on each subsequent venture. We've seen too many entrepreneurs become enamored with their success that they feel they can do no wrong in starting another venture. Let me remind you of some very salient points.

Let's not forget all the mistakes you made in getting your business off the ground. These lessons either cost you time or money but most likely both. Nevertheless they were important steps in becoming successful. And let's not forget about the people you hired or contracted who advertised themselves as one thing and turned out to be something totally different. How often did that set you back? And finally, let's not forget how many times you thought about quitting right before a major breakthrough happened which allowed you to keep pushing forward. Shall I go on?

We can say unequivocally that these things will happen again to some degree with more unknowns to pop up and grab you by the ankles. This should not be a surprise to you at this point. You will have to dedicate a considerable amount of time to get this new venture moving on its own. It's not much different than what you did to get the first business going.

Before you create another stream of income you must make one vital purchase: a learning curve. Buying a learning curve in any new venture is in essences buying yourself time to make mistakes before you have to rely on the results. Too often we risk too many resources on a venture long before we had a chance to practice and perfect our new methodology.

This lesson could be best understood by illustrating a cartoon I use to watch as a kid: Tarzan of the Jungle. In this cartoon, you'd see an animation of Tarzan swinging through the jungle from one vine to the next. He would grab one vine and then swing to the next vine. And once he has a firm grip, he releases the vine behind him in order to move forward in the jungle. If you pause the cartoon at a particular point, you would see that he has two vines; one in each hand. But once he knows the vine in front of him is strong enough to carry his weight he would release the one behind him so that he could move forward.

When seeking additional cash flow the above animation applies. Remember that you can't take your entrepreneurial hands off of a stream of cash flow until you know the new venture can hold your weight (deliver consistent revenue). Better said, you must give it your undivided attention until you know that it can consistently throw off cash with minimal effort from you. In this same cartoon, Tarzan once grabbed a vine that couldn't hold his weight and fell to the jungle floor. In reality that means your new venture may fall to its financial death carrying you with it.

Another example of buying a learning curve can be seen in real estate. I've seen people take the cash flow from their primary business and buy multiple distressed properties to rent out. They did this long before they learned the proper due diligence and property management techniques. This shotgun approach has cost them large amounts of money and time because they didn't allow themselves a learning curve. Here is an infallible rule: *the learning curve will take place whether you practice or use real money, so please take time to practice.*

As an option trader, I perfected my system and practiced with virtual money for over a year before I used my dollars. My friends would push me to use my own money early in my process but I refused to listen to them. They said things like "you have no confidence in yourself" or "if your paper trades are making money then use real money to make some serious cash". They had no knowledge of trading and they didn't understand my learning curve. When I was ready, I didn't lose money, get discouraged or give up quickly because I took the time to perfect my craft. Another rule: *you never want your learning curve to be longer than your money so please be patient as you go down this path.*

As the expression goes, *"for everything there is a season"* and this applies to business as well. In graduate school, we were taught about the life cycle of business:

1.) <u>Birth Stage</u>: When your mind conceives the business and you do what's necessary to have a grand opening.

2.) <u>Survival Stage</u>: When you do everything to bring revenue in the door. You become the chief cook and bottle washer. You craft deals just to get the sale.

3.) <u>Success Stage</u>: Things are going well and cash is flowing.

4.) <u>Decline Stage</u>: The old way you've been doing business no longer yields the same financial result. You begin to lose customers, competition becomes fierce, attracting & keeping talent becomes more difficult.

We won't delve too deeply into life cycles because they are self-explanatory; we want to focus on the seasons of your business and how they all have some seasonality to their cash flow. If you own an ice cream shop you will most likely see a drop in revenue during the winter. And a ski resort you will most likely see a drop-off in revenue during the warmer months.

If you look at your business as having four seasons you can equate the cycles this way:

1.) <u>Winter</u>: Business activity is at its lowest level of the year because decisions are not being made as frequently.
2.) <u>Spring</u>: Sales pipelines are expanding and customers have committed to making decisions and sales are picking up.
3.) <u>Summer</u>: Sales are at break-neck speed and you are doing all you can to keep up.
4.) <u>Autumn</u>: A quantifiable slow down in sales activity.

Now these seasons have no correlation to an actual calendar and a stage may last longer than three months, or sometimes less. Nevertheless, each business will experience some form of this cycle in a fiscal year period. Simply chart your sales or statement of cash flow and you will see your trend.

In our consulting business, we would see a significant drop in sales right before the summer months because decision makers don't make decisions before their impending vacations. At the Young Explorers Schools, summer months have slightly lower enrollments because parents plan along a normal school calendar: September to June.

Every business has these cycles and they could have a major impact on your cash flow. Some entrepreneurs may simply account for this by adjusting their overhead to lower costs (employee hours, supplies, training, etc.) And while doing so, they make adjustments to their lifestyle by not spending as much money as before. I'm not saying that it is wrong to be frugal; it's just that we don't believe in scarcity.

Believing in scarcity is the most limiting thought you can have and it is the genesis of any fear you can conjure up in your mind. You should have what you want and we don't want you to live beneath your means, just simply raise your means to meet the lifestyle you desire. This is the time and the opportunity for you to unleash your creativity and increase your means.

Most of the successful entrepreneurial couples we know believe in the concept of multiple streams of income; of leveraging their assets and expertise to bring more cash into their lives. They are always looking for new ways to do this and the ones who have mastered this concept never have a season to their cash flow.

Rita and I have talked with couples we know and have discovered some common trends. When these people chose another activity to stream income they follow a few simple rules:

Rules for Streams of Income

1. Never consider expansion of the current business another stream of cash flow.
2. Always leverage the assets you currently control to make another revenue stream.
3. Seek first to educate yourself on the new venture before you dedicate time, energy and resources (learning curve).
4. Find a coach with experience in the new venture before you dedicate major resources.
5. Understand the critical hurdles to success with quantifiable "Go/No Go" levels.
6. Clear exit strategy.

Keep in mind this will be an additional business for you so all rules apply to this venture as it did to your primary one. Here are some of the businesses that other married couples have incorporated into their strategy of multiple streams of income.

Real Estate

The real estate business seems to be the area of choice for almost every entrepreneur that we know; and it happens to be our choice as well. We chose real estate because of the tax benefits as well as the cash flow.

Experience has shown that your level of cash flow in real estate is determined by your level of expertise in acquiring the real estate. It is not only the price that determines the desired revenue stream but the terms, location, number of units, management, unrealized value and other things that come out through your due diligence. Bringing in the right people during the due diligence can assure you that the right decision will be made.

We started with a duplex in a decent neighborhood with two tenants to pay the mortgage. If one unit was vacant, then the other unit could pay the mortgage. We duplicated that success with more properties added to our portfolio. Our next step is to graduate from multiple single-family homes and step up to apartment complexes (100+ units) where we can use leverage for even more cash flow. Multi-unit buildings will necessitate professional property managers to increase the properties' value and rents. This will give us a consistent monthly income which is less likely to fall victim to seasonal trends.

When you bring in the right people and do your homework, real estate can offer many advantages. You may say that today's real estate prices are crashing all around us and it doesn't seem like the best investment. And our position is that you are both right and wrong. If you have no experience in selecting real estate you should either stay away or seek expertise. And for those with the right expertise, this is the best time to buy real estate that can cash flow for years to come. The best time to buy is when there is blood in the streets; we are fast approaching that time.

The advantage of real estate is that you can put down 15% on an apartment complex and the bank can supply the remainder. Your tenants pay the mortgage and you get to write off all the expenses while maintaining exclusive control over that property. It is paramount that you have exceptional management because your cash flow has a direct correlation to how well it is managed. A good property manager is always looking for ways to offer more value to the tenants; thereby increasing rents and cash flow.

Passive income from real estate also has tax advantages. Keep in mind that the payroll check you receive is taxed at the highest level. Uncle Sam just loves those working stiffs that have payroll taxes deducted every two weeks. Then the next level of taxes is on income you derive from the selling of stocks and other financial instruments. Here we are talking about short term and long term gains. And the lowest tax income is passive income which comes in the form of rents from commercial buildings, apartment buildings and office buildings. We like real estate because we like paying less tax on that cash flow. And when the market turns around, we are able to participate in the appreciation tax free. Maybe we'll get a line-of-credit on that building to buy another property?

You should talk to your coaches and mentors to find out what real estate investments they have. Ask where you should get started to educate yourself in this area of investment. We've found that our lawyer has many contacts in real estate and knows of properties that maybe open to a purchase. Select a good agent with a CCIM (Certified Commercial Investment Member) certification to find you additional opportunities in real estate. We have discovered that these individuals are worth knowing.

When it comes to our investment strategy in real estate for Young Explorers, we own each and every property our business occupies. We have separate corporations for each property for protection reasons and we pay rent to ourselves from one corporation to another. The real estate corporation charges the highest allowable rent for the area to the operating corporation. And then that entity writes it off as a business expense. The rent received by the real estate corporation is taxed at a lower rate then it would have been if we received it as earned income from the operation entity.

Don't let the current economic environment stop you from pursuing the right property. It's true that residential real estate has falling significantly with some more distance to go. And it's true that commercial real estate is feeling some of the same ill affects of this new normal but there are opportunities abound. Doing your homework is more important than ever but the upside is still great.

Intellectual Property

Do you recall one of the rules for multiple streams of income; *always leverage the assets you currently control to make another revenue stream.* With the real estate in the business you can take out some of the equity to acquire other properties. But this continuous chaos that we are currently in has reduced most of our equity to nothing, so what options are left? There is another asset you may have that you aren't aware can be leveraged; intellectual property.

When our accountant conducted a seminar on this we thought that we shouldn't waste our time attending. We didn't have any intellectual property because we just had a bunch of schools. We knew that the Montessori methodology was intellectual but that wasn't ours. We were positive that this concept didn't apply to us, but on a whim we decided to attend. The question that was posed to us was *"other than the physical things that you can touch in your business; what else does your business own?"* If there was something that wasn't physical, what was it and what value could it possibly have? As time went on, we finally understood the concept and started on a new path to another stream of income.

We found out that our intellectual property were things like our logo, taglines, brand, curriculum and our methodology for delivering that curriculum. Another form of our intellectual property was our business system which was the heart of Young Explorers. Within that business system was everything from how to select a location, architectural plans for our brand, accounting, marketing, human resources, etc. But how can you leverage this into another stream of income?

Well, the first thing we did was to setup a corporation that became the owner of all our intellectual property and the schools paid a royalty fee to use it. This royalty fee became a quasi source of income with significant tax advantages only. But it was so small that we had to look for other ideas.

This new way of thinking about intellectual property was one of those crawl/walk/run scenarios for us and we weren't even near the crawl stage. We decided to test the value of our brand first by using our logo because of requests for our customers. A customer wanted us to embroider a backpack with our logo so that her daughter could show neighbors her school pride. There was such a buzz that we offered them for sale to our customers and allowed them to purchase them on line.

To our surprise we started getting non-students asking if they could purchase backpacks. These kids became walking billboards for us within their elementary schools and our unsuspected business expanded. We later went to baby blankets and winter hats that were sold by an embroidery shop on our behalf. This became another stream of income we never thought could be realized.

Because so many people were buying our school gear without really understanding who we were, we started to generate a lot of curiosity. First, we started to notice that we were having people tour our school who didn't live in the neighborhood. The rule is if you lived more than five miles from our schools you probably would not enroll, so this was definitely odd. And the number of hits to our website was on a gigantic stair step climb over a one year period. Something was going on.

We then had two separate lawyers approach us on behalf of their clients and asked us if they could be a franchise school. What? We weren't looking to franchise and we didn't know the first thing about franchising. This is exciting and we are just now starting down that path and the intellectual property makes that a reality.

We are discovering the potential income stream of franchising our business system to others via our intellectual properties corporation. This will allow us to use minimal effort to control our brand while leveraging a monthly royalty fee. One of our friends owns a franchise from a famous fast food chain and explained how it worked. The chain sweeps money off the top line of their revenue stream every week and then charges them a fee for their supplies, marketing, food, etc. We are working with our advisory team to see the potential of this idea as we write this book.

Investing

What a broad topic for another stream of income. Up to this point, you've already been an investor. You've invested time and money in your current enterprise and it has returned a tidy sum to you every month in cash flow. So, suffice it to say you are already an investor and now its time to invest outside your business.

The genesis of our education on this happened when we read "Rich Dad Poor Dad" back in 2000. The author talked about the different categories of investors as listed below.

- *Accredited Investor*: someone with a net worth over $1 million, not including her home.
- *Qualified Investor*: similar to accredited with the ability to use certain financial instruments like hedge funds.
- *Sophisticated Investor*: $2.5 million plus in net worth with considerable experience in pre-IPO securities that are considered "non-prospectus" issues.
- *Inside Investor*: someone who is inside the investment and has some level of control of the business.
- *Ultimate Investor*: Takes his company public and sells to shareholders.

These categories gave us reason to hesitate and ponder what we wanted. Understanding financial instruments such as hedge funds and pre-IPO securities was not in our wheel house. Though our financial advisor said we were ready to be investors in some of these categories; it didn't excite us. We felt he would take our money and be the active participant at this level: not us. We like being in control of our own investments.

We wanted to be active investors in business and not necessarily financial instruments. We had years of experience in business and had the war wounds to prove it. That had to be worth something? And it was because of our resolve that we found a category that we could start with: Angel Investor.

- *Angel Investor*: an affluent person who provides capital for a start-up business usually in exchange for convertible debt and/or ownership equity.

We could seek out and make ourselves available to people with good ideas and strong work ethics who wanted to start or expand a business. We wanted to be for others what we desired when we first started: a place to get capital and coaching. We know that one of the biggest stumbling blocks to starting a business is lack of money. It has caused the early demise of many good ideas.

But when you take this path of angel investor, you must keep in mind that due diligence is the most important thing that you will do. You are investing money in someone with minimal business experience and/or a short record of success with the product or service, if any track record at all. To some this is considered a gamble. But to the experienced business person who has done the proper homework; it could be considered somewhat of a pre- IPO.

This avenue of income is not for the faint of heart and you will not hit it out of the park with each investment. We've discovered that most of these people lose more than they win, but the winners can make a nice cash flow for a considerable amount of time. Please recall our lesson on a learning curve; give yourself time to learn this area of business before you push all your chips to the middle of the table.

A good place to start is SCORE.org. Here is a place where you can leverage your past business experience to serve promising entrepreneurs. You will be volunteering your time but you will be surrounding yourself with like-minded people who will value your input. You may find a venture that you can invest in and take to the next level. No guarantees just possibilities.

You may do the same things with small business incubators. These groups normally have funds that they give to young businesses with the most promise and they are looking for experience business people to assist in the due diligence of these companies. Normally, these small companies have industry specific expertise but not a lot of capital or business experience. This is where you can add value and reap some rewards. If you are looking for another revenue stream, this has proven to be successful for many experienced entrepreneurs.

Another form of investing that has yielded a steady flow of revenue is in understanding how to trade stocks and other financial instruments. I will be the first to say that this can be a very frustrating endeavor to take on. And if you are emotional (like me), you must first learn to control your emotions otherwise you are destined to lose. Here is another learning curve.

We moved in the direction of trading option contracts on stocks because we loved the leverage. When it comes to business, we love two things more than anything else: leverage and cash flow. And our wealth has increased as we learned to master these things. When we trade stock options we use leverage by controlling a large number of stocks for a finite period of time for a very small investment. Yet we get to participate in the movement of that stock's appreciation in the multiples. It's not uncommon to place $500 on an option and get $1,800 in less than 5 days.

We've had this level of success on a consistent basis but it has come at a cost. Like with anything that you chose to do in business, you need to get educated. And after we received our education we practiced with "virtual money" under the guidance of a coach. We did this until we solidified our trading system. But there was a time that I got caught up in emotions early in this process and hit some major losses because I didn't work the system.

It became an obsessive rollercoaster ride filled with euphoric highs and manic depressive lows…and I'm not kidding. I would trade an option and win big and go on my high only to make another trade and lose even more than my earlier successful trade. I would get that gambler's mentality of "I've got to get my money back" and quickly seek out a plausible trade based on emotions. This would only lead to even more losses till I had to run to my bedroom, draw the blinds and hide from the world. Boy did Rita make fun of me when she saw me in that state.

I learned from my coach how to trade and succeed while still having a life by working my system and eliminating emotions. I learned how to do conditional trades where the trade would only be made if all my parameters were met. And if there weren't met during the course of the day; the transaction would die and the trade would never take place. I also learned how to do "covered calls" which allowed me to make a rental income on the stocks I already owned.

Mastering "stops" allowed me to walk away from Level 2 streaming quotes at the bottom of my PC screen and do other things. Before I was glued to my PC or smartphone watching my stock go up and down with each second of the day. Rita believes that is the reason I began to lose my hair and I believe that she's right. Now I put my trades in before I go to bed and an alert is sent when the trade is made. When I'm stopped out of a trade in a few days, I simply collect the money and I'm on to the next trade. Please don't be discouraged if it doesn't make sense as you read this. This is a new concept for many so training will be necessary; we just want to give you our experience so that you can determine if this maybe a viable path for you.

To continue, I started my education when I read a book by Dr. Alexander Elder call "Trading for a Living". It gave me a rudimentary understanding of what it took to consistently make money in trading stocks. From there we signed up for a class with an internet site called Investools®. A friend took this course and demonstrated to us what he learned and how his trades bought him a motorcycle. We wanted to use that same education to leverage only assets that would generate more cash flow so we could buy more assets (though a motorcycle is very cool).

I will make this disclaimer; this path works for us and it may not work for you. You have to determine how much time and money you are willing to put into this area of investment. I have to admit that this was, and still is, the longest learning curve compared to anything we've learned in business. But when you consider the leverage and the immediate cash flow, I would say that you would have to seriously consider this as another form of revenue stream.

Mom & Pop's Key Points:

1. Multiple streams of income will smooth out the seasonality of different businesses.
2. Real estate is still a great avenue for an additional stream of income; do your homework.
3. Learning to be an investor will keep you flowing in cash for generations to come.

Mom & Pop's To Do's:

4. Look into local business incubators to see how you can serve. Always choose to serve first and then you will be served.
5. Invest in learning about stocks, options & commodities. Read books from Jim Rogers and Dr. Alexander Elder.
6. Understand how precious metals preserve your purchasing power. We don't endorse numismatics, only bullion. Search the internet for James Turk, Michael Maloney and Eric Sprott.

A GIVING STRATEGY

As we write this chapter, I can't help but remember how I started down the path of entrepreneurship. It started with the exercise of understanding my Wealth Logic and how it had been perverted in my younger years. My upbringing gave me the perception that rich people were stingy, greedy people. And as I grew older I came to realize that most charitable contributions are made by those same people I deemed to be the greedy rich.

Most rich people have already learned the lesson that we were beginning to understand in earnest. My early belief was that money was power and the rich had all the power. But the true lesson is that money only has power in the way you use it. When you have money you have freedom with your time and we discovered that our time is even more powerful than our money. These are thought patterns that will become apart of your DNA as you become a successful entrepreneur.

In our mastermind group, we learned how wealthy people make giving a priority in their success formula. When we got together to discussed business ideas and how we could help each member achieve their goals, one of the most important agenda items was how we would share our success with others.

Now, I knew that this group of people was caring and giving because of the commitment they made to each other's success. But I had no idea of how important giving would be. Each couple in the group would outline their giving strategy and look for our guidance and suggestions. There were things like building an orphanage in Mexico to developing a foundation to assist kids with their college education; all fantastic ideas.

The first time I attended a giving session, I sat there quietly with my mouth slightly ajar. I remember whispering to Rita, "They're talking about giving it away before a single dollar comes in the door." This was such a shift in my thinking that it took quite sometime to get used to it. It's not that I'm a selfish person it's just that I don't think of how I'm going to share the wealth until I get the wealth. Rich people think totally different from the masses on many issues and this one is no exception.

As I changed my warped view on rich people early in my maturation process, I started to see many examples of how the rich would share their success. I look at people like Bill Gates and Warren Buffett who have taken most of their wealth and put it in charitable foundations to help those who are less fortunate.

Now, some may question their motivation and that somehow these people must win in this whole thing. Otherwise, why would they do this? And for those who chose that argument of cynicism I would simply ask you to look at your Wealth Logic. Your suspicion maybe based on your past mental programming. This would be an excellent time to stop and re-evaluate this mental block.

Let me nip this in the bud by saying "SO WHAT"! When there are people in need, sick children or a natural disaster trust me when I say that the needy will not deny a helping hand if the proper intention isn't there. Help is help and money is money. And if we can put it to good use so that all can be served, then that is money well spent. So if you are one of the few that are still harboring that sentiment; please release it.

Giving is the cornerstone of every successful person in the world. And for those who don't learn to develop a giving strategy; well their success becomes their prison. They don't see the value in giving so they take their wealth and use it to develop barriers between them and the world around them.

I recall a story told by Bob about a gentleman who sold his software company to a big corporation for millions. Not too soon after the news got out in an article in the local business paper; his phone began to ring off the hook. There were calls from financial planners, lawyers, charitable organizations, young entrepreneurs and alike. Then family and friends (or should I say Phamily & Phriends) began to pursue him because they had no idea of how successful he was until the news got out. Up to that point he lived a very modest life with a reliable car and small home.

He soon became paranoid and somewhat of a recluse because he felt the need to stay away from the vultures who wanted to pick his bones dry. He sold his small home to buy a bigger one in an exclusive gated community. And with phone numbers and email addresses changed he practically fell off the social grid in his community. Rarely seen and when seen; rarely spoke to anyone. This story was told to remind me of how the power of money can turn on you and hurt you.

We always say that the most important things to master in the area of business are leverage and cash flow and a giving strategy fits perfectly along side those two. We look at money as something that flows down the pipe of abundance. And it is not for you to hoard because it then becomes limiting. Allow us to use the analogy of a river and a land-locked pond to demonstrate the importance of giving to your wealth strategy.

As you develop multiple streams of income they become somewhat like rivers flowing cash into your home reservoir. The home reservoir is what pays for your home, business, investments and lifestyle. When you need to get money you simply grab a bucket and go to the reservoir to get what you need.

We know the value of the resource of money so we use it wisely and we teach our children to use it in the same manner. The reality is that this resource doesn't truly belong to us and those who don't believe this become greedy and their judgment becomes cloudy. This leads to bad decisions and a fast separation between you and your money. We're merely custodians of the resource so we work diligently to build out flowing channels of cash to other entities (i.e. charities) that could use it properly. We've developed systems to gauge each river coming in and going out so that all needs can be met without undue burden on any entity. This is one of the virtues of a good custodian.

If you have managed this process well, you will constantly receive fresh cash into your reservoir. Keep in mind the analogy mentioned above. When water stands without movement, as in a land-locked pond, it becomes stale, stagnate and useless. Scum tends to grow on the surface and mosquitoes start to lay their eggs. Very soon the water gives off a foul smell and becomes a problem.

Money works the same way; if it doesn't keep moving then it becomes stale and stagnates when inflation erodes its value. Then the mosquitoes, known as taxes, fees and thieves use your money for their purpose; taking more value away from you. This is what normally happens when you let you money sit in a checking, savings or money market account. You get a rate of return that is lower than the inflation.

If you let your money flow to your land-locked reservoir, then stagnation and erosion will happen just like a pond of water. This is why we advocate building rivers on both ends of your reservoir so that your outflows can serve more people and not become stale. As for our family, we have developed out flowing rivers of cash, or pipes, to causes that we feel can make the most impact in the world. Our churches, charity hospital, children's funds in and outside of the U.S.A. are some of our passions. We are also committed to small business incubators and financial education for youth.

As your business grows and you develop multiple streams of income, the pipe's diameter will expand to bring more cash in your direction. And though what we are about to mention is not an infallible rule in the eyes of most, it is in the eyes of the wealthy. It's like the law of gravity in that it cannot be broken under normal circumstances. And that rule: *To the degree you give of your time and money to a worthy cause, to that same degree you will be rewarded.*

We've seen this phenomenon in our lives on a consistent basis. It became very clear early in our relationship that Rita had a big heart for sharing and giving. Next to my mother, I don't know of a more caring and giving person in my life. During our deepest financial problems when I was trying to do everything to cut corners to keep the lights on and make payroll, it was always Rita's mantra to keep our giving strategy untouched. So we developed a few rules when it comes to money in our business. I must remind you that we developed these rules when things were going well:

Money Priorities for our Businesses

1.) *Make sure your business is cash flowing ASAP.*
2.) *Pay ourselves first; no matter what the business dilemma.*
3.) *Pay our giving partners second; no matter what the business dilemma.*
4.) *Pay for investment in other streams of income third; no matter what the business dilemma.*
5.) *Pay your creditors last with what is leftover.*
6.) *Never borrow money to pay bills. Create more revenue from the business.*
7.) *Be thankful for the opportunity to serve.*

It takes trials and tribulations to see if your rules and values can pass the litmus test. When I heard the train of financial disaster coming fast down the track of life, I wanted to quickly abandon virtue and go into survival mode.

Rita never took care of the books, so when said to hold the course on our money rules all I could say to her is "you just don't know how dire it is". She didn't know the details about our financial situation and it wasn't her job to know. It was her job to hold steady to the vision and the mission and let me sweat the financial details. And let me tell you; she made me sweat it out.

All things being equal, it was her faith that got us through those times. What we were doing in our business was apart of a higher calling. And just as important was her faith in the people and the causes we decided to give our money and time to. But what kept us moving forward was her faith in God. And the knowing that our business was His business and that the Lord never fails.

It is our faith that tells us it's incumbent upon us to give when much has been given to us. We are fortunate to be in a circle of entrepreneurs and business people who feel the same way. Getting back to the infallible rule we discovered; we have found that we have been richly rewarded in every aspect of our lives when we make giving a priority in our business.

Giving has turned out to be an investment that pays dividends in ways we cannot always measure. Through my wife, I found that when we continue to give during the rough patches; things get better. Now I'm a guy who tries to find the cause and effect in every business activity from marketing campaigns to adding brighter lights in the hallway of a building. But I cannot find an algorithmic pattern of cause and effect in this part of our strategy. All I can say is that when we give, things continue to get better in every aspect of our lives.

When you work your giving strategy you meet other giving people like you. This inevitably becomes the beginning of synergism for other great business opportunities. Some say that when you are doing God's work, He will reward you with His earthly and heavenly riches. We know, by faith, that there is much truth to that premise as well.

Others say that the act of giving is such a positive force that it rubs off on everything you do. This puts a silver lining on some of the occasional missteps in business. We know that positivity is a force multiplier that can get you through the crucible with the hope of better things to come. No matter what logic you prefer to use to substantiate the effects of giving, the conclusion is that giving makes all things better.

A LEGACY:
YOUR CHILDREN'S FINANCIAL EDUCATION

As I mentioned in an earlier chapter, you have to be on guard for the "P" Scoundrels. One of those would be the Posterity Scoundrels with your children as potential candidates for this group.

All of us as parents want to give our children everything that we didn't have growing up. Most of us, who started from very humble beginnings, have been thinking this way forever. As for me, it started at age 16 when I didn't have a car to drive to school like some of the rich kids who went to this all boy's catholic school I attended. I would say that my sons will not have to go to school without a nice car to drive.

Do you know what the most screwed up thing about that thought was? I was having it long before I got married and had my first kid. Poor me; deprived of all the necessities of life and at such a young age all because of my perceived lack when growing up. But what a blessing because it was that perceived lack that sparked my desire to succeed and have a better life.

Now that we have kids we know that if you give them everything you didn't have then they won't have anything to strive for. Some of us would call these types of kids privileged; we call them spoiled. They feel entitled to everything they want without any effort. They never learn how to handle the disappointments that come along with maturing into adulthood.

We made it priority #1 to teach him to work for what he wants. We are responsible for creating an environment that could ignite his desire and determination but he must work for it. This clarity came once he started school because it was all too frequent that we heard him say "I want a _ _ _ _" (fill in the blank with anything) because his friends had one.

That wasn't the problem because it's okay to desire things but the problem was when he said to us, "we're rich so we can afford it".

Then I would say the same words Bill Cosby use to say to his children, "your mother & I are rich; you are poor." We wanted him to know very early in life that it was up to him to get what he wanted in life and it was our job to equip him with the tools to do it.

As we mentioned in an earlier chapter, our sons fully understand that our money is not their money and that they should not expect a trust fund to finance their lifestyle. At first, our oldest thought it was a punishment and that we didn't love him, now he understands that it is a lesson on the journey to manhood. When he became 12 years of age we gave him a job cleaning the schools and some of our properties. And one day we started a conversation while I was reviewing the accounts receivables at one of the schools. He was whirling around me picking things up and vacuuming the rugs. This pivotal conversation was the beginning of his learning journey.

"Son, you forgot those papers there; please put them in the garbage", was all I said without giving him one glance. There was no reply but I could see out of my periphery that it was being done. A few minutes later I said, "Son, it would be nice to dust the director's desk; can you knock that out" and again no glance but this time I could tell he was moving slower than before. Raising a kid, you tend to pickup on their tendencies and their non-verbal queues and I gathered that he was upset.

"What's the matter Anthony"? I said with a curt tone. We made eye contact and he said absolutely nothing. I stopped what I was doing and I asked him to talk to me. I reminded him that work is not punishment; it just has to be done. He said to me "It must be punishment because I'm always doing the work and you're constantly telling me to do more". Now back in my day, these words would have never come from my mouth when talking to my father. As soon as the last word past my lips; I would have felt a firm fist in the center of my chest. But these were not the mid 1970's and I knew that this was an opportunity to coach him.

He said that it appeared to him that he did all the work and that I did nothing. He felt that the things I did at my PC and in my meetings was no more than "kicking back" and relaxing because I wasn't sweating like him. At that moment I decided that he needed a break and we drove to a nearby restaurant to have a drink and a father-to-son talk.

"Son, work comes in many different forms all of which add value to the world. You simply have to make the choice as to what kind of work you want to do", was how I started our conversation. "But Dad, you don't do any work at all" he said with a little smirk trying to dig a response out of me. "And I didn't choose this work; you chose this work for me and it sucks. When are you going to treat me like a man and let me make some choices?' was his retort. I could see the tears beginning to well in his eyes and I wanted this conversation to have a positive impact and not push him away.

I told him that life can be just like me in that it may make you do a job that you don't want to do. As a child, you must do what you're told by your parents until you mature and develop the knowledge to make your own choices and step out into the world. But if you get older, and not mature, you may still find yourself living in your parent's house and living by their rules. You'll feel that your parent's are treating you like a child by giving you curfews and chores, but you have to abide by their rules until you step out into the world on your own.

If you don't mature in knowledge, namely business and financial knowledge, life will make you do the jobs that you don't want to do. And it doesn't matter that you're eighteen years old and considered an adult, life will still make you do work you don't want because you haven't matured. This immaturity will haunt you everyday of your life and you will know it when you have to get up early for a job you hate, take directions from a boss you don't like or respect and receive a meager salary that doesn't allow you to live the life of your dreams. Soon you will realize your future is dim and you've lowered yourself to a state of just existing.

"Well I guess there's no difference between you and life and I'm just stuck doing something I hate till the day I die" was his mellow-dramatic response. What a knucklehead! If he was looking for pity or poor victim sympathy he was surely talking to the wrong parent today. "There are two things that are absolutely wrong with your statement. First, life doesn't love you but I love you with all my heart and I promised the Lord that I would coach you through life….and I will do that until my last breath. Secondly, you are not powerless in life; you have all the tools to create whatever you want. And that includes the work you do".

His response was, "I'm still stuck doing garbage pickup and cleaning rooms". And I told him that he must continue doing those jobs as apart of the maturing process. Learning how to do the tough things you hate are important markers on the way to achieving a very important goal. I talked about my experience working for UPS in college and how I loaded semi-trucks each night as a way to make ends meet. A conveyor belt would send a package down the line to me every four-seconds and those packages were sometimes 50+lbs.

I would sweat so much that I would walk out of the facility each night with squishy sneakers filled with my own moisture. What I learned from that experience was what I didn't want to do for the rest of my life. And I believe that he was well on his way with the same lesson. To get to the point where you can do the work you want, and make the money you want, you must grow in maturity and knowledge.

"Well Dad, I see that you don't do the kind of work that I do, nor the kind of work that the employees do, so what kind of work do you do?" I tried to explain to him that his mother and I had decided to take the path of entrepreneurship in lieu of a career path. And that we use the tools of leverage (other people's money and other people's effort) to grow a business that can serve our customers, employees, giving partners and our family. Through creativity, knowledge, vision, communication and coordination, we drive our business systems to reach our goals and we don't have to do the traditional work that you are doing.

He admitted that he didn't understand a single thing that I was saying but wanted to learn more because he wanted to do other things in his life. He made me proud because that was an adult thought coming from the mouth of a pre-teen. We then mapped out a process for him to increase his knowledge of business so that he could not only serve the family business but serve his own business ventures as he became a man.

Critical Factors in Financial Education for Youth

1.) Involve them in the business
2.) Play the game of investments (Monopoly® and/or Cashflow®)
3.) Invite them to business meetings (vendors, BODs, coaches)
4.) Teach them to read financial statements
5.) Teach them to sell

Involve Them in the Business

There is no education better for your children than to get them involved in the family business immediately. We made it clear to our sons that we all had a responsibility to the household and to the business. That meant at home you must do your chores and in the business; you must do your job. There was no negotiation on compensation or what needed to be done because it is your duty as a family member. I said no negotiation in compensation because this is the first issue to come up with any employee and it doesn't matter if they're family or not. Primarily for the sake of his education, we took compensation requests off the table.

The importance of working in the family business is to serve and to learn and getting some cash is secondary. This was a big hurdle for my oldest son to jump because he felt an hour of work necessitated and hour of wages. Giving money to our children for every effort given tends to cloud the learning process when it comes to money. We had to find the opportunity to teach him that working for money is a long path to financial freedom. But coupling hard work with a firm financial education will get him to his goal quicker.

This brings to mind a time when he was determined to get a long board skateboard (I have no idea what this was but it is what the kids like to ride). The investment was going to be about $225 and he had a timeframe of immediately. There was some big skateboard event with racing and tricks in our neighborhood in less than two weeks and he had to be there with the new board. He posed the question to us about how he could earn that money ASAP. He had asked the right question.

We knew it would be a challenge to earn that much money doing extra work in the business in such a short timeframe. It would take many hours each day; more than he was use to doing. He was on summer break and to him, each day was precious and he didn't want to spend the whole day working. But we set forth a list of duties for him to perform to make the money. He earned the money, bought the board and sped to the event.

What was odd was he came home about an hour earlier than planned. We guessed that he didn't perform well or maybe some altercation took place at the park and he felt it necessary to come home. He went straight to his room and within minutes we could hear him snoring. The next morning when he came down for breakfast we asked how it went. He explained how he used both his boards in some contests and learned some new moves but he was just exhausted before it was all over. He had worked his butt off on everything we listed for him plus added chores around the house to earn that money.

"Hey Dad, how can you enjoy the nice things you work for if all you do is work and you're exhausted? I don't like being too tired to enjoy that board I bought", he said. Here is a lesson that was juxtaposed to what we learned as children, but he had stumbled upon it now and it needed to be addressed. He was about to learn about leverage again.

We told him that having a job means that you have to work before you get paid. But when you own a business you can participate in cash flow from the work of others. Wealthy people don't work for money instead they put money to work for them in their business, real estate and investments. Each dollar becomes an employee and at the end of the day, those dollars bring home more dollars. I said to him. "That is why the rich can skateboard all day a never get tired; funny huh?" He didn't see the humor at all. When you learn how to leverage other people's effort your workload will decrease and your cash flow will increase.

When you involve your children in your business, you are able to teach them how to start and run a business. They learn how to use leverage in order to get more out of the business with less of their effort. Learning the value of a hard day's work is good for the soul and has great biblical meaning. But once the lesson of hard work has been learned then it's time to put your assets to work to get an even greater return. "I see now Dad that it's not that you don't work it's just that you work differently. That's good stuff." This statement was proof to us that we were getting through to him.

Play the Game of Investment

Our sons love to play games. Our oldest is skilled in athletics like football & baseball and loves to compete with me when possible. Rita has taught him chess and I taught him to play Texas Hold'em poker, all of which he has become very good at doing. On many occasions, he's given her a run for her money in chess and has beaten me in poker as well. Nothing gives that kid more joy than giving me a thorough beat down in the contest of his choice.

When he was about eight years old, we acquired a property and put it in a LLC (Limited Liability Corporation) named after him and his brother. He later stated that if I named the company after him then he must be the one who owns the building. Nice try son! He kept demonstrating interest in what this company did and how it made money. We later explained to him the game of investing and like the other games and sports that he played; it involves skill to be good.

"Oh, if it's a game, then once I learn it I will be able to beat you at it", was his typical cocky response to anything that concerned competition with me. I've always loved his confidence and I told him that it was "game on" once he learned some skills. Now the first place we went to start his training was in the hallway closet high above the coats and hats. The box was old and the corners were held together by some masking tape, but the contents were still good enough to teach the lesson.

The game of Monopoly® was where we learned our first business lessons as kids and it's still relevant today. He wanted to learn how real estate works as an investment and Monopoly has been able to show him just that. He learned the concepts of owning the right property (he felt orange properties were the best) and getting the highest possible rent for that property. As he got better, he mastered the concept of leveraging the bank's money to get more property through a mortgage. And yes, he was able to beat me in no time flat.

We encourage you to play games like this, as well as Cashflow® from the Rich Dad Company. He has become so enthralled that he plays both games on-line. It appears that kids today would prefer to use electronic devices and the internet to get to these games. Nevertheless, the education about how money makes more money can be had no matter the old board game or not.

Now that he is a little older, I've let him in on the details of managing rental properties and selecting properties for triple-net leases (NNN). He is learning the process of due diligence on one-family and two-family rentals. Understanding all the costs and revenue stream helps him better value the property and what he should pay for it. He is also learning to screen tenants and understand his rights in the leasing documents; all of which will help him become a better real estate investor.

But don't let their investment knowledge stop at real estate because there are many more vehicles to prosperity. If you have learned how the financial markets work then expose them to it as well. Understanding how to select stocks and going long (buying) or shorting (selling) can be a great form of appreciation and future revenue. And using options and or futures can be an even better avenue of cash flow. But in this area, you need to build this investment muscle over time and not expect results immediately. Most young people today have a comfort level with everything electronic; so we've set up virtual money accounts for him to trade stocks and build this skill.

Invite Them to Business Meetings

What a valuable experience for your children even if they find the thought extremely boring. It began for us on a snowy Cleveland morning when school was cancelled because of a snow storm. Rita had a doctor's appointment and I had a morning meeting with our banker and an afternoon meeting with our accountant. I took the youngest to Young Explorers and under much vocal protest; took my oldest with me. Playing video games and texting were the preferred activities for him on snow days, so I made an offer. If he would attend these meetings with me I would let him snowboard that evening; and the deal was sealed.

In my first meeting, we drove to the bank to discuss refinancing options on a few properties as well as line of credit for a new project. During the meeting my son was pretty much heads down listening to his ipod® until he saw the numbers written on the whiteboard. "Excuse me, but this bank is going to give my Dad that much money?" He said with an astonishing tone. Here is where I let my banker take over.

The two had a brief dialogue on how bankers helped small business owners finance projects and the bank was somewhat of a partner. Not a partner in the traditional sense because the bank didn't share in the profits nor the appreciation, depreciation, tax advantages, etc. All the business owner had to do was make the monthly payment (debt service) every month and the relationship was good. Even more important was that the bank wanted to be apart of every project we did because of our successful track record.

We left the meeting with my son asking a boat load of questions about how this bank could help him start a snowboard business. His mouth was moving a mile a minute and I'm sure his brain was moving even faster. He thought it was great that the bank would give him money so he could make more money. It appears the concept of leverage was taking root in my son's budding business acumen. "Who else do I need on my team to start my snowboard company Dad?" Well, we were on our way to see the accountant and that maybe another team member.

We had a quick lunch and headed over to see our CPA. He is also an entrepreneur with many properties and a trucking business that he sold to his sons as apart of his exit strategy. Let me say that it is invaluable to have an accountant who truly understands business, not just debits and credits. As we sat down in this meeting I noticed that Anthony didn't have his headphones on this time. He actually bellied up to the table in the posture of an active participant.

This was our quarterly sit down to talk about anything new that could affect our year-end tax situation. We talked about a strategy of paying ourselves less to lower our federal tax and floating more through our passive income entities. We talked about forming a new Series LLC in another state for our intellectual properties like our curriculum website called The Lesson Box.com and this book. We addressed forming entities offshore as a tax saving option. All of which my son seemed to follow very well. We then talked about how our cars were about to come off their leases and it was time to seek new transportation.

Our accountant thought that we should go ahead and lease two new vehicles and expense through the business. Since the majority of its use will be in the business, we could write-off a major portion of all expense. Again, my son found an opportunity to jump into the conversation, "Are you saying that my snowboard company will pay for my car and it will be free for me to use?" I took a brief moment to explain the background behind the outburst and how we just left a meeting with our banker. Our accountant is also one of my coaches, so he took this opportunity to teach my son on how using the right accounting methods could leverage your money, assets and time. He talked about how cars, meals, trips could all be legally expensed if done properly. Anthony also asked about expensing snowboards and other equipment and he gave him a strategy that made him smile.

On the snowy, slow drive back to our side of town the questions began to fly as fast as the snow was falling. When you spark the imagination of a child nothing can hold them back. He mentioned that he understood how a business, if run well, can take care of his lifestyle. It was clear how the right teammates can make you successful as well. He used analogies in football and baseball to demonstrate his understanding; sports that he has been playing sense he was five years old. But what I found even more refreshing on the ride home was that he said that he no longer felt I didn't work. He felt that what I did in the business team was important even though it didn't seem hard.

"Dad, you are the head coach in the business just like when you coached me in football and baseball", was his realization. Okay, I wasn't quite sure of his logic but we still had some windshield time till we got home so I let him continue to talk uninterrupted. He said the head coach is the guy who selects his assistant coaches and his players and decides what positions the teammates will play. In his eyes, I did the same thing in the business by selecting my coaches, employees, managers, accountant, banker, lawyer, etc. Then I decide what role they will have in the business such as being merely a vendor or a strategic partner or coach.

And like a football head coach, you look at the situation on the field and determine what play to run. Do you go for a sure thing like a 3 yard run up the middle to get a first down or do you go for the long bomb to win the game? As a business leader, you may decide to do the sure thing like marketing a new service to your existing customers or go for the bomb in buying a new facility to expand the business. "The way I look at it, you have the hard job of making the right decision on the big stuff. That's your job and I wouldn't want that right now", is how he ended his monologue.

Wow, either I'm a great teacher or he's just gifted with clarity of thought. Either way, he managed to distill it down to a level that most adults could not do. This epiphany didn't happen overnight; he's been drenched in this mode of thinking sense the day he was born. The point here is that you must expose your children to your business and let them attend your meetings. They will learn what you do and be able to offer value to the business as they mature.

Teach Them to Read Financial Statements

Anthony laid on the kitchen counter a printout of his Spanish score in a school academic challenge. The scores were in a combination of numbers, letters with Greek letters and it was all written in Spanish of course. I could faintly hear him and his mother talking about it while I was in my den about two rooms away. Her tone revealed that she was very pleased with his results. Hey, I like to share in my kid's achievements too so I walked into the kitchen. They quickly disbanded into different areas of the house (this happens to me all the time).

I picked up the document and walked toward my son to congratulate him on doing so well. But as I looked at the documents, I didn't understand a single thing on it because I don't speak or read Spanish. He said to me, "Thanks Dad, but you don't know what you're reading do you? He knew the answer to that question. "How do you know it's a good score or a bad score if you can't read it Dad?" He was absolutely correct! If you can't read a report then how can you determine what is good or bad?

Every business and every property has a report card just like my son's academic challenge score but it means nothing if you don't know how to read it. A business' report card is a series of financial statements that tells you how it's doing and they are crucial to making a good business decision. Here are the critical financial statements:

Critical Financial Statements

Statement of Financial Position: Balance Sheet
Statement of Comprehensive Income: Profit & Loss
Statement of Cash Flows: Cash flow activities

A balance sheet is a simple document that tells you the financial condition of a company by showing you what the company owns (assets) and what they owe (liabilities) and the difference is what's yours (equity). My son equates this to the preliminary physical that he takes every year before he goes on a week long Boy Scout campout. It tells you the health of the company in a snapshot manner. If debt levels (liabilities) are high that tells you that the patient has something wrong with him and he may need a thorough physical to determine the problem.

If your company, or a company you plan to purchase, show similar maladies, then you should dig deeper into other financial reports to better ascertain the problem. As an exercise for my son, we looked at the balance sheet of a company that we considered buying. Within 15 minutes of looking at the balance sheet and doing a quick ratio.

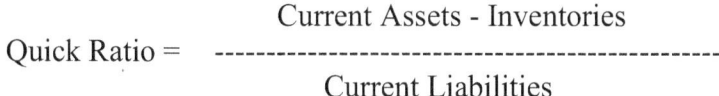

$$\text{Quick Ratio} = \frac{\text{Current Assets - Inventories}}{\text{Current Liabilities}}$$

He ascertained that this didn't look good. The ratio was too low based on our requirements. He didn't know much more than that at the time but he was building knowledge and confidence. This empowered him to dig a little deeper to find out why.

The P&L statement (profit & loss), also known as the income statement helps us better understand how a company buys and sells its product and service to make a profit. He compares this statement to a report card with a GPA at the bottom line. In school, all the grades come together to give you your GPA but some grades are weighted differently by credit hours. Some classes are worth one credit hour; some others are worth three or five credit hours.

Continuing the parallel with your P&L, you may find that your grade on landscaping expense is below par because the expense is higher than normal. But because it is landscaping, it's weighted lower than other expenses (landscape expense = one credit hour) and has a smaller impact on the bottom line. In the same instance, you find that the payroll expense grade is also slightly below par but because salaries are weighted very high (salary expense = five credit hours) and its impact to the bottom line is far greater. The same rule applies to the different products or services that make up your sales. Sales of one widget maybe weighted lower than the sale of a different widget.

Even though your GPA is pretty good you know that a slight up tick in activity within a highly weighted subject can take you from a B+ to an A-. That could mean a higher GPA and in business parlance; that could be a better P&L statement.

Then there is the most important statement of business, or at least in my mind; the cash flow statement. Envision cash as the life blood of your business because without it your business will meet with a quick demise. And your business system as the heart that pumps the blood; refreshing it with the oxygen of new customers, products and services on a consistent basis. In the process of doing your due diligence on this financial report, you are like a heart surgeon looking closely at the EKG before deciding on the remedy. Okay, I maybe taking a little more literary license than I deserve but I do this to demonstrate the importance.

The cash flow statement best describes how cash flows into and out of your business; it is the difference between just being able to open a business and being able to stay in business. When we study the movement of cash through your business, called a cash budget, we can determine patterns of how you take in and pay out money. The goal is to maintain sufficient cash for your business to operate from month to month. Anthony was responsible for operating his personal business based on cash flow because his cell phone bill was due monthly and he had to earn enough every month to stay current.

Teach Them How to Sell

The most important skill you can teach your young entrepreneur is to sell; bar none. She can be mediocre in all other areas of business but if she becomes a true sales professional; the sky is the limit. Okay, I know what you're thinking; salesmen are slimy, sneaky swindlers. Those descriptive terms can be applied to a select few in all professions but there is one thing about sales people that is universally true: *Nothing in the business world happens until someone sells something.*

My first sales manager at Xerox would tell us this all the time. This was back in the 1980's where JIT (Just in Time Manufacturing) was all the rage. And at Xerox, a copier wouldn't be built on the factory floor unless a salesman had a signed order for said product. So the statement above was absolutely true. And if we didn't sell enough products, not only would you put your job in jeopardy, but the jobs of all the factory workers, support and administrative staff. What a heavy load for most but not for the seasoned sales professional.

Without exception, every successful entrepreneur I've ever met was a good salesperson; consciously or unconsciously. They are always selling if not to the banker for financing or a vendor for preferred pricing; then they're selling a customer a product or an employee on going beyond the call of duty to reach company goals. Trust me when I say you are a salesperson. And I would say that you are pretty darn good one if you've gotten your business to the point that you are coaching your children on financial acumen.

As early as possible, get your children to sell something. For us it started with our boys selling candy bars and popcorn for the Boy Scouts. They slowly whittled away at their fear of rejection. Mastering the fear of rejection is a stage all entrepreneurs go through so why not start them as early as possible. Make them accountable for their results and what we mean by that is; don't sell for them. Don't buy all the candy and popcorn and donate to the office so that they can meet their sales quota. You are not serving them one bit because you are denying them the opportunity of figuring it out.

After a few bloody knuckles earned from knocking on doors, bring them into the business and let them witness you selling or your best sales people. Sit down with her after each sells call and ask her some questions:

What did you like about the sales call?
What were your goals going into the sales call?
What did you accomplish on the call?
What were the objections? How did you overcome them?
What was exciting, scary or disappointing about the call?
How would you rank my performance on the call?
How would you handle the call differently next time?

Their answers to these questions will give you a better idea of what should be next in their learning process.

Mom & Pop's Key Points:

1. Stoke the flames of desire; don't give them everything.
2. Take them on as many business meetings as possible.
3. Make teaching sales techniques a high priority.

Mom & Pop's To Do's:

4. Play Monopoly & Cashflow a couple times a month.
5. Review your financial statements with them and ask them to uncover areas of improvement.
6. Encourage them to launch their own business during their free time (cutting lawns, babysitting, etc.)

EXIT STRATEGY

In the basement of a young artist's home, he had delivered a huge block of marble. This marble was very expensive which required a substantial amount of his savings to purchase. He had a full-time job but took classes in the evenings to perfect his artistry skills so that one day he could become a great artist. So, at each lunch break, he would take out his sketch pad and plan out the sculpture that he wanted to create. He would then periodically meet with his art teacher to review his sketches. Together they would make sure that he was incorporating all the proper principles that were crucial to sculpting a masterpiece.

Then one evening, he firmly took his hammer and chisel in hand, took a deep breath, and made his first mark on the pristine block of Italian marble. The moment was marred with anxious anticipation and excitement because he made the tough decision to make his dream a reality. For years he spent evenings and weekends toiling away in his basement making this beautiful piece of art. And occasionally he met with roadblocks and unforeseen difficulties in his creative process.

There were veins of clay and sand in the marble that could not be seen when he first took on the project. These imperfections were in areas of the marble that were critical to the creation of the sculpture. One miscalculated strike of the hammer or placement of the chisel could sever an important part of the marble and it would land on the floor in a heap of disappointment. At these times, the young artist would go to his teacher and strategize on how to handle the problem and still create the desired sculpture. The guidance would allow him to minimize all the mistakes a young artist will sometimes make on such a huge project.

Then one day he gently smoothed away the last piece of marble to reveal the most beautiful piece of art that he could imagine coming from his heart, head and hands. He pulled out his sketches to compare the final masterpiece to what he had planned years ago.

And to his amazement, it was far more detailed and more beautiful; it was finally finished. So what does he do next?

This story of the artist is no different than your story when you've created a successful business. Most likely, you started this business in your basement, spare room or kitchen table. It was done on nights and weekends so that it would not interfere with your primary employment; which paid the bills. Of course, you worked on it diligently to put your own unique fingerprint on every aspect of the business. But like the artist above; there comes a time when the business you created is done and you have to make a decision.

The young artist could decide to keep the sculpture or lease it to the local art museum for all to pay admission to see. This would give him a monthly revenue stream for the foreseeable future. Or he could sell it to an art collector who would give him top dollar for his creativity. And this could finance his lifestyle for a while as he tackled his next art project.

There is an old saying when it comes to your business, "If you don't sell the business when it is done, you're buying it all over again". When you buy something you have to operate it, maintain it and insure it. But when you sell it; that part of the business is no longer your concern. The thought of an exit from the business was so overwhelming to my wife that just the mere mention of it would cause her to roll her eyes and ignore me. She would always say the business was like her baby and she couldn't bear to separate with her baby.

My reply was that our business didn't come through her birth canal, though the pains in the beginning were almost as intense. So if you want to compare the business to our children, then let's complete the analogy. Keep in mind that children are born to leave; it may sound harsh but it's true. When they grow up, they no longer need you and leave home to seek someone else to partner with to start a new life. I say our business must do the same. Though my logic was perceived to be initially warped, we all agreed that once it was finished that it would have to be sold and leave our lives.

Now, most exits have been carefully planned out to the minutest detail, yet there are times when life events happen and that may hasten your exit. We call these the Dooming D's of the Exit.

The Dooming D's of the Exit

1. Divorce: when your marriage dissolves then your business will suffer many ramifications. It would be foolish to not discuss this with your spouse, but we believe a business built on a firm foundation of a covenant will make this less of a possibility.

2. Disability: this could have major financial constraints on the business. And if the disabled partner is considered a "key man", this may affect the business' future.

3. Death: this can be just as devastating as divorce.

The intend of this book is not to handle what we call forced exit strategies brought on by the life events listed above, but they do need your attention. We recommend that you sit down with your attorney (maybe a trust wealth protection specialist) and map out an insurance plan under these scenarios.

Listed below are some potential strategies for your planned exit.

Potential Exit Strategies

1.) Sell (employees or investors)
2.) Succession Plan to Children
3.) Franchise

Selling the Business

When the business is finished then it will be time to sell it. But how do you go about it? How can you make sure that you are getting the right offer? These are some of the questions that will race through your mind. But remember that this exit has been planned carefully since the early days of your business success. You always start a project with the end in mind. So this step should not be a surprise yet that doesn't in anyway lessen the emotions that come along with this stage.

First thing to do is to prepare your mind for this major move. I've been told that the major life events are: divorce, illness, job change, death and relocation. Well, I would like to add selling a business as a major life event. It's normal to go on an emotional rollercoaster ride with a lot of ups & downs during this process so rely on your team to help you through this. Your team of coaches & BODs were there as you grew this thing and will be there as you exit it. These professionals tend to be less emotional and should assist in those areas where your emotions may get the best of you.

Secondly, sit down with your accountant and do a proper valuation of the business. That means the real estate (if you own it), other assets, trademarks, goodwill, intellectual property, receivables and everything else. She can give you a detailed analysis and make recommendations on what you can do to increase value prior to selling. They can set your expectations on what multiples of net earnings you can expect in an offer. Depending on the business, you may see 2 – 3 times net earnings in an offer or you may see up to 4 – 8 times net earnings. Starting here with your team will prove to be the best use of your time.

Then there will be time for serious tax planning because you are about to have a major tax event in your life. You should sit down and do "what if" analysis on what will happen at the time of sale. And how you could change your tax structure now in anticipation of sale. Is the sale going to be an asset purchase or a stock purchase? What assets will you keep and which ones will be included in the sale? If real estate is involved then you may consider a 1031 exchange to lower tax burdens. Planning is what lowers your biggest expense (taxes) and with a major capital gain, you will need some planning.

Thirdly, contact your commercial real estate professional. This may not seem very obvious to you if you want to sale your business but I want to share something here. Commercial agents are sales professional and birds of a feather flock together. If these people don't already have an expertise in selling businesses then most likely they know professionals who do. Similar to how a residential real estate agent can evaluate a home you want to sale and give you suggestions on staging it for an open house; these acquisition professionals can do the same.

After an agent has signed a non-disclosure, they can look at your business, your operations and your financial books to further refine your value. They can then offer suggestions to increase value, but more importantly, they can submit offering memorandums to qualified buyers. And they know who the qualified buyers are.

Lastly, please consult your attorney. When you get further down the road of selling your business, you will begin to see large documents come by your desk. They will have titles like "Letter of Intent", "Asset Purchase Agreement", "Acquisition of Interest Agreements" and "NNN Lease Agreement", etc. These documents are normally submitted by the buyer's lawyer and are designed to protect the buyer. It will be your lawyer's job to review and make revisions to protect you and your interest. If you've picked the right attorney for your team, he will demonstrate his value immediately.

Earlier we were discussing the option of selling to an outside investor, but you should also consider selling to your employees. This is a little trickier and we recommend that you get the proper advice before you move forward. Some have converted their companies to ESOP companies (Employee Share Option Plans) in which the employees buy the stock of the company over a period of time. We only know of one instance in our circle where the owner had no family members to give the business to and he chose this option. He valued his management staff and wanted them to continue the business in his absence. Please research this further as it maybe an option for you.

Succession Plan to Children

There will be that group of business owners who will sell their business to their children. Now, I did say SELL and not GIVE the business to their children. We've met many people who said that they will never give their business to their kids. But teach them how to operate it, grow it and then allow them to purchase it.

A succession plan must be to adult children who know the business, have been taught how to run the business and have a desire to continue to run the business. If any of these factors are missing, you are in jeopardy of sending your business to death row and having your children resent you.

First, evaluate your children's ability to run the business before you exit. For most businesses, the adult children would have gravitated to those areas of the business that they love or have shown a proclivity to add substantial value. It would be fair to assume that the years would have groomed them to be very proficient in those areas. So if you want this business to continue to grow so they can all have a great lifestyle and offer the same opportunity to your grandchildren, then you must evaluate them stringently.

We say that you must send your children through the same vetting process that you would if you were hiring a non-family member. If you have multiple children then evaluate them for multiple positions with one question in mind; what is the best decision for the business? One bad appointment of a child could kill the livelihood for the rest of the siblings, as well as make Thanksgiving dinner somewhat tenuous.

If you find that your child doesn't possess the talent to fill your role as you exit, then you must go outside to find the right fit for the job. You must set an environment that will allow this person to have all the rights, duties and privileges that come along with that position. And you must set barriers so that your children cannot thwart the power of the position. We have seen parents hire a president to run the family business prior to their exit and that person was not a family member. It happens more often than you think. Suffice it to say that these businesses have continued to grow and the siblings are happy with the company's success.

Now, let me get back to the original premise of this section. The owners who exit should consider selling the company to their children; not give it. We recommend that you make your children buy shares in the business in their earliest days of full-time employment in the family business.

If they chose to stay then you should encourage them to buy more and if they chose to leave; then they can sell it back to the company. We know of one family where two kids didn't want to be in the business but wanted to keep their shares. The parents converted their shares to non-voting shares and limited their ability to affect the company's direction.

This sets you up for a fast exit by allowing them to buy out all your shares or a major portion. Under this scenario we've seen some do a gradual exit to make sure that the company is in the right hands. We met a couple that owns a metal tube company and they slowly exited the business over a two year period while handing over the reins to their sons. The sons initially bought 30% of the shares and then 49% of the shares.

When mom & dad felt confident in the sons' abilities, and the team they built around then, they sold them the remaining shares. Took a large part of the proceeds to invest in apartments and commercial property and they are living off the incoming rents. He compared it to teaching them to ride a bike when they were young. He jogged behind them with is hand on the backseat until he was confident they could ride on their own.

Franchise

"When you franchise, you are still in the business and you have not exited", was what Rita said when we were first approached with this option. We spent years developing a franchise model business system that could work even when we weren't there; but we never considered actually franchising. And I must admit that I agree with her in this matter; in a franchise we would still have to work it.

When a franchise has been implemented properly, you can truly minimize your contact to as little as quarterly meetings. This may be difficult at first but if you've put the right people in place, it will run smoothly. When I say the right people in place, I'm talking about a President and all her staff to make the business run. This team will do the day-to-day stuff, as well as an executive team to make strategic decisions and grow the business.

This doesn't sound like an exit yet does it? Most of us think that an exit means "take the money and run". Well this exit is a little more akin to an annuity where you are paid monthly for as long as the business is running. And if things go according to plan, this annuity will pay out to you far more than a one time lump sum amount.

And you still have the option of a permanent exit because you can sell it an outside investor or to your executive staff at anytime in the future. This method will just allow you the ability to receive your cash flow for a little longer with minimal effort.

We've come to the end of your business and the end of this book. Your prize at the finish-line is a large amount of money and a large amount of time. You've made the long climb up this mountain to the summit and you are taking it all in. Take a breath and enjoy all the great views around you. You've learned so much and giving so much, now before you do anything else, you may decide to sit back for a long moment and enjoy what you've accomplished. You can count yourself among a very rare fraternity of people who have started a business, grew it and sold it for a handsome profit. Yet you are still full of great ideas and motivation to succeed so you maybe asking yourself this rhetorically. But if not, then we will:

WHAT ARE YOU GOING TO DO NEXT?

YOUR BUSINESS IS YOUR
ONLY LINE OF DEFENSE

We wrote this book for a few reasons. First to let you know that currently you have very few arrows left in your quiver to slay the deadly dragon that is stealing your wealth. You can call it anything you choose; the government, the unions, the banks, the Chinese, etc. It really doesn't matter which one you chose because in our opinion this monster is a multi-headed beast representing all the entities we just mentioned. And they all work together in taking away your wealth. No paranoia here and no conspiracy theory just look at the price of food, gas and your taxes to gauge your movement up the prosperity ladder.

Let's take a close look at the working middle-class in the US. We are slowly becoming extinct because inflation and taxes are pushing our purchasing power lower and lower everyday. Corporations are finding ways to increase their bottom line without taking on more employees; while some are sending jobs overseas. This is putting many families firmly into the lower class of American society; none of us should be there.

We want to reinforce the idea that entrepreneurship maybe the only way to grow your wealth as an American citizen. As we mentioned in the book; being an employee you are taxed the most and you have the least power to change it. It's okay to keep your day job and blaze this trail in the evenings and on the weekends. And it's okay to dedicate the efforts of one spouse to the new venture while the other handles the day job. There are many paths to success, just don't be afraid to tackle them.

We don't know you personally but we know the type of person you are. You are just like us…maybe more unique in ways you don't realize yet. Nevertheless, you desire more than what the corporate rat race has offered you at this point. And we're confident that you have the desire in your heart that will drive you until your vision is realized. Yes, I would say that you are a lot like us.

So get your ideas on paper and do your homework. Conquer that negative self talk and confront your PWL. Read books about business and your favorite business icons. Invite other entrepreneurs and professionals into your world and take heed of their counsel. You are well on your way to a new life - a better life.

We invite you to visit our website to get ideas and encouragement. You can also blog with others like you in their various stages of entrepreneurship. We invite you to evaluate us as your coaching team. We have been coaching others for the last four years and maybe we can help you. We are very diligent in our process of selecting apprentice couples and we only have time for a few. Leave a message at our website and let us know how we can serve you.

Prepare your heart and minds for a fantastic ride and I'm certain that you will create a business that will serve many and fulfill your dreams. And when you arrive to your destination, we will count you as one of us, one of many, From Mom & Pop to Millionaire.

www.mompopmillionaire.com

www.ingramcontent.com/pod-product-compliance
Lightning Source LLC
Chambersburg PA
CBHW051529170526
45165CB00002B/659